Choosing
CONFIDENCE

3-MINUTE DEVOTIONS
FOR TEEN GIRLS

© 2022 by Barbour Publishing, Inc.

Print ISBN 978-1-63609-434-2

Scripture quotations marked CEB are taken from the Common English Bible® Copyright © 2010, 2011 by Common English Bible,™ Used by permission.

Scripture quotations marked CEV are from the Contemporary English Version, Copyright © 1995 by American Bible Society. All rights reserved.

Scripture quotations marked AMP are taken from the Amplified® Bible, Copyright © 2015 by The Lockman Foundation. Used by permission.

Scripture quotations marked NCV are taken from the New Century Version®. Copyright © 2005 by Thomas Nelson. Used by permission. All rights reserved.

Scripture quotations marked NLT are taken from the Holy Bible. New Living Translation copyright© 1996, 2004, 2015 by Tyndale House Foundation. Used by permission of Tyndale House Publishers, Inc. Carol Stream, Illinois 60188. All rights reserved.

Scripture quotations marked VOICE are taken from The Voice™. Copyright © 2008 by Ecclesia Bible Society. Used by permission. All rights reserved.

Scripture quotations marked NIV are taken from the HOLY BIBLE, NEW INTERNATIONAL VERSION®. NIV®. Copyright © 1973, 1978, 1984, 2011 by Biblica, Inc.™ Used by permission. All rights reserved worldwide.

Scripture quotations marked GNT are taken from the Good News Translation® (Today's English Standard Version, Second Edition), Copyright © 1992 American Bible Society. All rights reserved.

Scripture quotations marked MSG are taken from THE MESSAGE, copyright © 1993, 2002, 2018 by Eugene H. Peterson. Used by permission of NavPress. All rights reserved. Represented by Tyndale House Publishers, Inc.

Published by Barbour Publishing, Inc., 1810 Barbour Drive, Uhrichsville, Ohio 44683, www.barbourbooks.com

Our mission is to inspire the world with the life-changing message of the Bible.

Member of the
Evangelical Christian
Publishers Association

Printed in China.

APRIL FRAZIER

Choose
CONFIDENCE

3-MINUTE DEVOTIONS
FOR TEEN GIRLS

BARBOUR
PUBLISHING

Introduction

Here is a collection of thoughts from the true Source of all confidence and encouragement—God's Word. Within these pages you'll be guided through just-right-size readings that you can experience in as few as three minutes:

- Minute 1: Reflect on God's Word
- Minute 2: Read real-life application and encouragement
- Minute 3: Pray

These devotions aren't meant to be a replacement for digging deep into the scriptures or for personal, in-depth quiet time. Instead, consider them a perfect jump-start to help you form a habit of spending time with God every day. Or add them to the time you're already spending with Him. Share these moments with friends, family, classmates, and others you come in contact with every day. They're looking for encouragement and confidence too.

My heart is confident in you, O God; my heart is confident. No wonder I can sing your praises!
PSALM 57:7 NLT

Calm Confidence

This is what the Sovereign LORD, the Holy One of Israel,
says: "Only in returning to me and resting in me will you
be saved. In quietness and confidence is your strength."
ISAIAH 30:15 NLT

Daily you face the choice: Where will I put my confidence—in God, myself, or someone else? Are you looking to God to save you? Do you rely on yourself to get through? Or do you put all your hope in someone else, believing that person will save you? The Israelites said, "No, we will get our help from Egypt. They will give us swift horses for riding into battle" (Isaiah 30:16 NLT). They refused to rest in God's care for them, to calmly trust God for protection and deliverance. They took matters into their own hands and placed their confidence elsewhere. But our true strength lies in our calm trust in Jesus. What problems do you face today? Choose confidence in God.

Lord, today I choose to put my confidence in You,
not in myself and not in others. Help me face today in
calmness and peace as I depend on You to care for me.

What's Your Source?

Whom have I in heaven but you? And earth has nothing
I desire besides you. My flesh and my heart may fail, but
God is the strength of my heart and my portion forever.

PSALM 73:25-26 NIV

It's way too easy to be confident because of your looks, abilities, friends, followers, possessions, or anything else that makes you feel valued. Don't be tricked so easily! The source of your confidence is more important than your actual confidence. Placing your confidence in yourself or the things of this world will always let you down because those sources are unreliable. Place your trust in Jesus. Gain your confidence from Him. He will always be with you and never let you down. His strength will more than make up for what you lack. Be confident because you are created with the image of God stamped on you, because you are loved by God, because God knows you are beautiful, and because you have perfect protection, peace, and power in Him.

Lord, show me where I'm drawing my confidence
from people or places other than You. Help
me shift my focus to You as my source.

The Choice

Jesus said to all of them, "If people want to follow me,
they must give up the things they want. They must be
willing to give up their lives daily to follow me."
LUKE 9:23 NCV

Jesus requires that we give up everything to follow Him. That's a hard ask. Why do people willingly do that? It seems crazy! But when you are so confident in someone, you're willing to make sacrifices. You're certain what you will gain is far better than what you will lose. You're fully confident that Jesus is someone you can trust.

Do you have that confidence in Jesus? Do you know Him well enough that you're willing to trust Him with everything? When daily decisions require you to choose between your way and God's way, how often do you sacrifice what you want for what God wants? At times God's way seems hard and scary. That's when we must *choose* confidence. Knowing God's character gives us the confidence we need to walk in faith and obedience.

Jesus, I'm not gonna lie: You ask a lot of me. Help me know
You better so I can follow You with total confidence.

I Am

Moses said to God, "Suppose I go to the Israelites and say to them, 'The God of your fathers has sent me to you,' and they ask me, 'What is his name?' Then what shall I tell them?" God said to Moses, "I AM WHO I AM. This is what you are to say to the Israelites: 'I AM has sent me to you.'"

EXODUS 3:13-14 NIV

Names meant a lot in ancient times. They reflected the character and nature of the person (Genesis 17:5-6; 32:27 28; Matthew 16:17-18). When Moses asked for God's name, he was asking, "How do You define Yourself?" God said His name is Yahweh, which means "I am who I am," indicating God is not bound by time. He is eternal and independent of all creation. He always was, is, and will be (Revelation 1:8).

Our culture prefers to define God by its own terms. People choose whatever version of God is easiest to accept. But we must allow God to define Himself by what He has revealed in the Bible.

Lord, please reveal Yourself—who You really are—to me.

Unchanging

I am the LORD, and I do not change.

MALACHI 3:6 CEB

Change is part of our lives—and that fact won't change. From major world events to the stuff going on for each of us individually, change is a constant. Think about your own life: Friends come and go, and your friend group tends to change from year to year. Maybe you changed schools or switched to homeschool. Maybe you changed churches or your parents had to change jobs. No matter how you slice it, life has a way of looking different, sometimes overnight!

You know what's not different? God. "Jesus Christ is the same yesterday and today and forever" (Hebrews 13:8 NIV). He is the constant in the changing chaos. When you need a steady presence, a faithful friend, or unwavering advice, turn to Jesus. Choose to put your confidence in the unchanging nature of our reliable and trustworthy God!

Lord, all the constant change can make the world feel like it's spinning in chaos. Thank You for Your steady presence that centers me and calms me and guides me.

God Is Good

The LORD is good and does what is right;
he shows the proper path to those who go astray.
PSALM 25:8 NLT

The very nature of God is good. He is the ultimate standard of excellence, virtue, moral uprightness, and worthiness. "Taste and see that the LORD is good," said the psalmist. "Oh, the joys of those who take refuge in him!" (Psalm 34:8 NLT). The Bible testifies many times to the goodness of the Lord (2 Chronicles 5:13; Psalm 100:5; 106:1; Nahum 1:7).

Satan likes to sneakily whisper that God is *not* good: He can't be trusted. He's a stern judge or an abusive, absent Father who doesn't really care about you. Satan will use the failings of earthly fathers or other adults to distort our perception of God. We must recognize these lies and allow the truth to rehabilitate our view of God.

How are you tempted to believe God isn't good? Ask God to help you have confidence in His goodness.

Lord, help me taste and see that You are good. Correct my perception of You so I can understand who You really are.

Forever Faithful

If we are not faithful, he will still be faithful,
because he must be true to who he is.

2 TIMOTHY 2:13 NCV

We had a golden retriever while I was growing up, and she was the most loyal dog we ever owned. Wherever I went in the house, she'd follow. She was my pillow when I watched TV, my teammate playing in the snow, my protector at night. She never went to bed until I was in bed, and if I stayed out late, she'd wait in the hallway for me to come home. I could be rude, moody, or flippant to her, but she always remained faithful to me.

Jesus is the same. In His perfection, He can't *not* be faithful. It doesn't matter how faithful *you* are. You can have confidence in *Jesus'* faithfulness to you. He will never leave you or stop loving you—no matter how you treat Him.

Faithful Lord, please forgive me for the ways I'm
unfaithful to You. Show me how You want me
to change. Thank You for never leaving me and
for faithfully loving me—no matter what.

Always Present

"I am with you always [remaining with you perpetually—regardless of circumstance, and on every occasion], even to the end of the age."

MATTHEW 28:20 AMP

Jesus never leaves your side. Ever! He's *always* with you—when you're walking the halls at school, competing in an event, navigating fickle relationships, or feeling lonely and left out. He *sees* you (Genesis 16:13). He *knows* you (Psalm 139:1-4). You cannot hide from Him (Psalm 139:7-10). He's the ultimate best friend.

Don't let your feelings make you doubt the truth. We don't always *feel* like God is listening, that He cares, or that He's near. When those doubts seep in, kick those lies to the curb and repeat what you know is true! You can be confident that God is with you right here, right now. And He's staying with you until He comes back to take you to be with Him forever. That's a promise!

Jesus, thank You for never leaving me! Even when I feel alone, I'm not. Help me remember that. Thank You for never letting me face scary or hard things by myself. Your faithful presence brings so much comfort.

Creator

You alone are the LORD, Creator of the heavens and all
the stars, Creator of the earth and those who live on it,
Creator of the ocean and all its creatures. You are the
source of life, praised by the stars that fill the heavens.
NEHEMIAH 9:6 CEV

God existed before all creation (Genesis 1:1). God made the world simply by speaking it into existence (Psalm 33:6, 9). As Creator, God fully controls all creation (Daniel 2:21; Luke 8:24). There's a lot of buzz about the dangers of climate change, but the destruction of the planet will not take place until its appointed time (Revelation 6). We are to be good stewards of the earth and care for it (Genesis 1:28), but God ultimately controls the earth's destiny. We can rest in confidence that He is Lord of all creation, the source of all life, and He will protect and preserve it until He builds the new heaven and new earth (Revelation 21:1).

I praise You, Creator God, for all that You've made.
Help me care for Your creation yet relax with
peace that You are in full control of the earth.

Silent Testimony

*For ever since the world was created, people have seen
the earth and sky. Through everything God made, they can
clearly see his invisible qualities—his eternal power and
divine nature. So they have no excuse for not knowing God.*

ROMANS 1:20 NLT

All of creation clearly reveals the nature and character of God.
"The heavens proclaim the glory of God. The skies display
his craftsmanship. Day after day they continue to speak; night
after night they make him known. They speak without a sound
or word; their voice is never heard. Yet their message has
gone throughout the earth, and their words to all the world"
(Psalm 19:1–4 NLT).

The delicate bloom of a flower speaks of God's love for
beauty and creativity. A garden bursting with vegetables
proclaims God's ability to bring life from death: dead seeds
planted in the ground transform into living, fruit-bearing plants.

Look outside. What do you see? What does it reveal to
you about God?

*God, how amazing that all creation speaks of You
without saying a word! Help me stop and notice.
Help me have a deeper understanding of You
through observing Your handiwork around me.*

Slow to Anger

The LORD passed in front of Moses, calling out, "Yahweh!
The LORD! The God of compassion and mercy! I am slow
to anger and filled with unfailing love and faithfulness."

EXODUS 34:6 NLT

Satan loves to distort our view of God. One of his tactics is to make us believe God is an angry judge who sits in heaven and frowns at us all the time. You might laugh, but how easily do you believe these lies? "God is punishing me." "God is disappointed in me." "God is frustrated with me."

Because God is pictured as a Father, Satan also loves to mold your view of God the Father to match the imperfect example of your earthly father. If your earthly father abandoned you, abused you, or is quick to be angry at you, you may believe God the Father is like that too. But let the truth sink in: God is a God of compassion and mercy. He is *slow to anger* and filled with *unfailing* love and faithfulness!

Yahweh, reveal the lies I believe about Your
character, and help me remain confident that
You always view me with compassion and love.

God of Mercy

"I am merciful."
EXODUS 22:27 NLT

Theologians (a.k.a. really smart people) often define mercy as not getting what we deserve. We all sin, and everyone falls short of God's perfect standard (Romans 3:23). The punishment for our sin is death (Romans 6:23). Period. That's what we deserve. But God in His incredible love sent His Son to take our place (John 3:16). Jesus came to earth, lived a perfect life, and died on the cross—taking the punishment of death for us.

We've all had moments when we messed up big-time. We waited anxiously for the punishment we knew we deserved— and received mercy instead. That's just a small taste of the mercy God shows us. You can be certain God is not holding your sins against you or waiting to punish you for every failure. Yeah, you sin and mess up. But when you come to Him for forgiveness, He says, *"I am merciful. You are forgiven."* So live in freedom from guilt and with gratefulness for the amazing gift of mercy!

Merciful God, thank You for not giving me what I deserve! Help me show mercy to others in return.

Lord Who Heals

"I am the LORD who heals you."

EXODUS 15:26 NCV

"Dear Lord, please heal so-and-so who's sick. Help them feel better." How often have you prayed something like that? Probably a lot! There's nothing wrong with praying for physical healing—whether for small things like a cold or big things like cancer. But God heals in a much deeper way than just our physical ailments. He wants to heal us *fully*—emotionally, spiritually, and physically. He wants to heal your mind of all the lies you believe about yourself. He wants to heal your emotions and all the past wounds that keep causing you emotional pain. He wants to heal you spiritually—first through salvation by restoring your relationship with Him, then by healing all the misperceptions you have that keep you distant and distrustful of Him. Will you pray today and ask God for healing—true, deep healing—where you need it?

Lord, please heal me! I'm broken and hurting,
and I need Your healing touch. Heal the lies with
Your truth. Heal my brokenness with Your love.

God Who Sees

*She gave this name to the LORD who spoke to
her: "You are the God who sees me," for she said,
"I have now seen the One who sees me."*

GENESIS 16:13 NIV

Hagar was fleeing a desperate situation. Her mistress Sarai, not confident in God's promises, gave Hagar to her husband, Abram, so Sarai could have children through Hagar. The plan worked. Hagar became pregnant, but Hagar despised Sarai for it. In return, Sarai abused her so much that Hagar ran away. She was pregnant, alone, and in the middle of a desert when the Lord appeared. What did He tell her? Go back to Sarai and submit to her (Genesis 16:9). *What?!* Hagar had been sorely used, but the Lord would not abandon her. He promised blessing.

Hagar's encounter with God proved that He saw her circumstances and cared about her. Their meeting gave her the confidence to go back to Sarai and submit. Hagar knew she was not abandoned and alone. The God Who Sees Me stood beside her.

*God Who Sees Me, I know You care about me. Give me
confidence today as I face my own circumstances.*

God Our Helper

God is our refuge and strength, a help always near in times of great trouble. That's why we won't be afraid when the world falls apart, when the mountains crumble into the center of the sea, when its waters roar and rage, when the mountains shake because of its surging waves.

PSALM 46:1-3 CEB

Just watching news headlines for a single day shows a world falling apart. The fear and hysteria—this is a world without God. But we are not without God! He is our shelter, a place of protection we can rest under while storms rage. He is our strength; He gives courage amid all the fear. We don't have to be afraid because He is always near, always ready to help us.

You do not face this day—or any day—alone. Keep your eyes firmly fixed on Mighty God, not the world falling apart. God alone can give you confidence and peace. Let that confidence and peace fill you and shine through you.

Lord, I run to You as my shelter and help. Give me strength and courage. May Your peace flow through me to reassure and encourage others.

God Our Rescue

*"I am the LORD your God, who rescued you from
the land of Egypt, the place of your slavery."*

EXODUS 20:2 NLT

The Israelites lived as severely oppressed slaves to the pharaoh of Egypt. They lived in despair, depression, and bondage. They were stuck and had no way out—until God stepped in and rescued them.

We all have our own Egypts and places of slavery. How do you feel enslaved? What has a hold on you and makes you feel trapped and helpless? Are you a victim of bullying? Are you a slave to food, and you live in despair and depression about your weight? Are you a slave to popularity, and you can't make yourself leave the popular crowd? Are you a slave to fashion and beauty? A certain sport? An addiction? Call out to the Lord your God who rescues you from the place of your slavery! He will free you and guide you out of your Egypt if you're willing to follow Him.

*Lord, rescue me from my slavery! I can't
do it on my own. Guide me out of this pit,
and help me have the courage to follow You.*

Warrior King

"Today you're going to fight a battle against your enemies. Don't be intimidated by them! Don't be afraid! Don't run away! Don't let them terrify you! The Eternal, your True God, has come out here with you, and He'll fight for you against your enemies and save you."

DEUTERONOMY 20:3-4 VOICE

Sometimes just walking into school feels like entering a battle. Tension with friends or dealing with bullies makes your steps drag like you're trying to wade through water. You'd rather be anywhere but here.

Dealing with conflict is never a party. But you don't have to fear the battles because you're not alone. Jesus, our Warrior, walks with us, fights for us, guards us, and protects us. What battles are you facing right now? Are you running from them, or do you have the courage to face them confidently, knowing Jesus is by your side?

Eternal, True God, nothing can defeat You. Help me face my battles today. Give me courage and wisdom, and help me trust You to fight for me.

Mighty Defender

"So no weapon that is used against you will defeat you. You will show that those who speak against you are wrong. These are the good things my servants receive. Their victory comes from me," says the LORD.

ISAIAH 54:17 NCV

When you're on God's team, attacks *will* come. You can count on it. God has an enemy, and choosing God's side puts a target on your back too. But God doesn't leave us defenseless! Choosing God's side means you're also choosing God's protection. The benefits of being on His team include a Mighty Defender who will not allow the enemy's attacks to defeat you. The battle and victory don't depend on you—God's in charge!

When gossip and slander are aimed at you, pray before you quickly jump to your own defense. Let God guide you and fight for you. When you're accused unfairly, check your anger and turn to the Lord to vindicate you. It's not on you to fight your way out of attacks. Put your confidence in God and let Him battle to victory for you.

Lord, I put my trust in You. Please fight for me today and give me wisdom.

God with Us

For to us a child is born, to us a son is given.

ISAIAH 9:6 NIV

Think of a moment in your life when you really needed someone. . .and they came. The joy! The relief! The comfort and love. Humanity desperately needed a Savior. . .and He came. Jesus *came*! "Though he was God, he did not think of equality with God as something to cling to. Instead, he gave up his divine privileges; he took the humble position of a slave and was born as a human being" (Philippians 2:6-7 NLT). The divine Creator chose to be born to a poor family, in a smelly barn, with a feeding trough as a cradle. He saw humanity's great need—and He entered it in the humblest way possible. What a holy, simple, magnanimous moment!

Jesus sees your desperation and needs. Ask Him to come, and He will meet you. Whatever muck and mire you face, He'll step right into it with you. He *came*! For you.

Jesus, I worship You! Thank You for giving up everything to be born as a tiny human. For becoming like me so You could rescue me.

King Jesus

For a child is born to us, a son is given to us. The government will rest on his shoulders. . . . His government and its peace will never end. He will rule with fairness and justice from the throne of his ancestor David for all eternity. The passionate commitment of the LORD of Heaven's Armies will make this happen!

ISAIAH 9:6–7 NLT

Jesus is coming back! When He returns, He will establish a kingdom of perfect peace—no more wars or corruption (Zechariah 9:10). He'll rule with perfect fairness and justice. Everyone on earth will worship Him, and His kingdom will never be destroyed (Daniel 7:14). Sounds like heaven! Because it will be.

The world around us is decaying rapidly. Sin's ugly influence is everywhere. It's easy to lose hope that things will ever turn around or be fair or right. But they will be! God promises. We can keep our hope and confidence in Him. One day He *will* come back and restore all things.

Jesus, I can't wait for Your return! As the world falls apart, help me remain at peace, because one day You will make all things right.

Wonderful Counselor

For a child is born to us, a son is given to us. . . .
And he will be called: Wonderful Counselor. . .

ISAIAH 9:6 NLT

Sometimes you just need advice. Someone to talk to who gives you guidance and perspective—someone who's *not* your mom, you know?

Jesus is an amazing counselor. The Bible tells us, "The Spirit of the LORD will rest on him—the Spirit of wisdom and understanding, the Spirit of counsel and might, the Spirit of knowledge and the fear of the LORD" (Isaiah 11:2 NLT). He's one wise guy! And He loves to listen to you and guide you. So pour out your concerns to Him in prayer or in a journal. When you face a problem or wonder what to do, honestly ask Him for guidance. Then wait and listen. He'll answer you. It might take a while, but be patient and keep waiting and listening. You can be confident He'll answer—and His will be the best advice to follow.

Okay, Jesus, here's the situation. . . .
I need Your advice. What should I do?

Mighty God

For a child is born to us, a son is given to us. . . .
And he will be called: . . .Mighty God. . .
ISAIAH 9:6 NLT

The ancient prophecy of Jesus' birth clearly indicated that the Messiah would be divine by giving Him the title "Mighty God." Jesus, while fully human, was also fully God. Talk about a brain twister! But Jesus, the second person of the Trinity, is "the God of gods and Lord of lords. He is the great God, the mighty and awesome God, who shows no partiality and cannot be bribed" (Deuteronomy 10:17 NLT). No one and nothing is stronger than Jesus. No sin is greater than His forgiveness. No evil is greater than His power. No person or situation is beyond His redemption. No force can stand in His way. Nothing can stop His plans. He is Mighty God!

What in your life seems bigger than God at this moment? What are you tempted to fear more than Him? Ask our Mighty God to intervene, and put your trust in His power.

Mighty God, I put my trust in You and Your power.

Everlasting Father

For a child is born to us, a son is given to us. . . .
And he will be called: . . .Everlasting Father. . .
ISAIAH 9:6 NLT

Isaiah clearly prophesied about a son who would someday rule as a messianic King. The New Testament identifies this Messiah as Jesus. The title "Everlasting Father" isn't referring to God the Father here. This title is used to describe the Messiah-King as the protector and provider of His people. This King will rule eternally and be the compassionate caregiver to those in His kingdom.

We have the hope of someday living in Jesus' perfect kingdom forever, but He is still our Everlasting Father right now. How do you need Jesus' protection today? How do you need His provision? His tender care? Humbly approach Him with your requests. Your Everlasting Father delights to care for you!

Everlasting Father, I praise You for all the ways You've
protected me and provided for me. Thank You for
lovingly caring for me. Please care for me today by. . . .

Prince of Peace

For a child is born to us, a son is given to us. . . .
And he will be called: . . .Prince of Peace.
ISAIAH 9:6 NLT

Sometimes we just need *peace* in our lives! Peace at school, peace with our parents and siblings, peace about our future. A lot of times we try to create that peace by seeking control. If we can manipulate people or the situation, we think we can create the outcome we want. We often lose our peace when we feel like life is out of control. But being lord of our life and in control is not the true source of peace. *Jesus* is our peace. When you let go of control and trust Jesus with the outcome, you can walk in peace even if a storm rages around you.

Where do you need peace in your life? Invite the Prince of Peace to take charge, and be confident in the counsel He gives you.

Prince of Peace, forgive me for trying to create
my own peace by being in command. Your peace
is so much better. I surrender control to You.

Relational God

"The virgin will conceive and give birth to a son, and they will call him Immanuel" (which means "God with us").

MATTHEW 1:23 NIV

God's greatest desire has always been to be with us. He walked with Adam and Eve in the garden of Eden at the beginning of creation (Genesis 2:8). When sin wrecked that closeness, He drew near to humanity in other ways: leading the Israelites by a pillar of cloud and fire (Exodus 13:21-22), dwelling physically in the tabernacle and temple (Exodus 40:34-38; 1 Kings 8:10-11), becoming a man who walked and lived among us, and giving us the Holy Spirit who lives inside us (John 14:16-17). One day He will create a new heaven and earth where He can live with us forever (Revelation 21:3). Do you see how much God *longs* for relationship with you? He'll remove all barriers, fight any battles, and take any risks in order to be with you. You can count on it!

God, it's humbling to know You so badly want a relationship with me. Help me draw close to You too.

The Word

*In the beginning was the one who is called the Word.
The Word was with God and was truly God. . . .
The Word became a human being and lived here
with us. We saw his true glory, the glory of the only
Son of the Father. From him the complete gifts of
undeserved grace and truth have come down to us.*

JOHN 1:1, 14 CEV

Christian lingo says you need to "have a relationship with Jesus." But how do you have a relationship with someone you can't see?! And how do you know if it's God speaking to you or if it's the ham and cheese you ate for dinner messing with you?! Relax, friend. You can have a relationship with Jesus—even though you can't see Him—through His Word, the Bible. Jesus *is* the Word. The Word *is* Jesus. So know the Word. . .and you know Jesus. Spending time reading the Word is spending time with Jesus. The more you know Him, the more confident you'll be in your relationship with Him.

*Jesus, I want to know You better. Bless the time I
spend in Your Word, showing me who You are.*

Bread of Life

Jesus replied, "I am the bread of life.
Whoever comes to me will never be hungry again.
Whoever believes in me will never be thirsty."

JOHN 6:35 NLT

Jesus fed five thousand people with five loaves of bread. Hungry again, that same crowd went searching for Jesus the next day. Jesus scolded them for working so hard to find Him just for another free meal. He's good for more than a physical handout. When we seek Him with spiritual hunger, He will always satisfy us. (Read the whole story in John 6.)

Meeting physical needs is only a temporary fix. Our real and lasting problem is our spiritual state: Who will we depend on to find forgiveness, peace, and eternal life? Only Jesus can provide those things with an unending supply. Don't get me wrong, God loves to give gifts to His children and meet our physical wants and needs (Matthew 7:11)! But most importantly, we should seek Him with our spiritual needs. He is the Bread of Life, who can supply *all* our needs—physical, emotional, and spiritual!

Jesus, I come to You today seeking not just
physical things, but desiring You to feed my soul too.

Light of the World

*Jesus spoke to the people once more and said,
"I am the light of the world. If you follow me,
you won't have to walk in darkness, because
you will have the light that leads to life."*

JOHN 8:12 NLT

Without Jesus, we walk in spiritual darkness and death. But Jesus shines His light on our hearts so we can understand and know who God is and the path He wants us to follow (2 Corinthians 4:6). How do you need Jesus to shed light in your life? Do spiritual questions niggle and require answers? Are you struggling with a decision or situation and need some guidance? Are there secrets or sin you're keeping in the dark that should be brought into the light of confession and forgiveness?

Walking in the light brings freedom and blessing (Psalms 27:1; 84:11; 89:15). But, you ask, *how do I know what God wants me to do?* God's peace will guard you (Philippians 4:7). When God's peace fills you, you know you are walking in the light.

*Jesus, I need Your light today. Show me the
steps to take, and surround me with Your peace.*

The Gate

"I am the gate for the sheep. . . . Those who come in through me will be saved. They will come and go freely and will find good pastures. The thief's purpose is to steal and kill and destroy. My purpose is to give them a rich and satisfying life."

JOHN 10:7, 9-10 NLT

Jesus gave an analogy and compared Himself to the gate of a sheep pen. There's only one way in and out of that pen—the gate. Anyone who tries to climb into the pen another way only intends to harm the sheep (John 10:1).

Many people and religions offer ways to God—but they are lies intended to harm you, the sheep. Satan wants to rob you of the life Jesus offers. "Come out from the pen," he whispers. "This pen is too restricting. There's a better pen over there with more freedom! Ditch this place." But you can be confident the salvation Jesus offers is the only freedom and satisfaction you'll find.

Jesus, sometimes what the world tells me sounds a whole lot better than Your way. Help me recognize the lies so I can stay under Your life-giving care.

The Good Shepherd

"I am the good shepherd. The good shepherd sacrifices his life for the sheep."

JOHN 10:11 NLT

Jesus willingly died for you (John 10:18). The suffering of the cross was more bearable to Him than the suffering of being separated from you forever because of your sin. That's a deep love!

Because of that love, Jesus fiercely fights for you. When Satan comes sneaking around as a wolf in sheep's clothing, Jesus exposes the lies and frees you from harm. If Satan has led you astray, Jesus will search until He finds you (Matthew 18:12–13). Jesus is the Good Shepherd. He only wants the best for you. Will you come under His gentle care and let Him lead you today?

Jesus, thank You for caring for me so deeply. Thank You for always fighting for me, protecting me, and never leaving me. Help me see Your goodness and love when I want to struggle against You. Help me place my confidence and security in You instead of trying to do things my way.

The Resurrection and Life

Jesus said to her, "I am the resurrection and the life.
Whoever believes in me will live, even though they die."
JOHN 11:25 CEB

Mary and Martha, close friends of Jesus, sent word to Him that their brother was deathly ill. Jesus delayed coming to see them, and Lazarus died. When Jesus finally arrived, He found the sisters weeping in grief. This intensely moved and distressed Him (John 11:33). The original Greek word carries the meaning of anger: Jesus was deeply indignant or angry. At what? The sisters? No, death itself. He fumed about the tragic results of Adam's sin (Romans 5:12). He found Himself surrounded by the pain and consequences of Satan's evil— and He got *ticked.* "You don't get to win, Satan! I won't let you take them from Me," Jesus seemed to say. He brought Lazarus back to life, and He made a way for *all* of us to receive eternal life.

He defeated death forever (1 Corinthians 15:54-55). That's the God we serve!

God, thank You for the hope of eternal life. Thank
You for grieving with us and comforting us when
we face the physical death of loved ones.

The Way

Jesus told him, "I am the way, the truth, and the life.
No one can come to the Father except through me."
JOHN 14:6 NLT

Jesus stressed again that He's the only way to eternal life with
the Father. Why did He keep repeating that? We get it already!
But Jesus knew we'd need to hear it again and again—just like
your mom often tells you to do something more than once,
because she knows you're not really listening! In our human
stubbornness, we don't want to accept there's only one way.
We like to think we know better and can choose our own way.
But Jesus reminds us again: *"Nope, there's no other way but
Me."* You can fight it, deny it, and try to dance around it, but
there's the plain, simple truth that will never change. Only
His path is the right path. His truth is the correct truth. And
His life is the real deal that satisfies. Have you accepted that?

Jesus, I surrender to You my desire to go my own
way. Show me Your way and the life You offer.

The Vine

*"I am the true vine, and my Father is the gardener.
. . . I am the vine; you are the branches. If you
remain in me and I in you, you will bear much
fruit; apart from me you can do nothing."*
JOHN 15:1, 5 NIV

The key to success is surrender. Say what? You can pursue your own goals and dreams as hard as you want. But to truly succeed, it's not how hard we work for our goals—it's how well we surrender our desires and pursue what *God* wants. We can do nothing apart from Him. Anything we create or build ourselves apart from God is empty and meaningless.

To find lasting fulfillment, we need to learn the art of abiding in Christ—looking to Him for love, direction, and satisfaction. When we submit ourselves to God's way, our lives will blossom with incredible fruit. How well are you abiding in Christ? What distractions need to be pruned out of your life that are keeping you from receiving the life-giving nourishment of Jesus the Vine?

*Jesus, help me remain in You today. To let
go of my agenda and be in tune with Yours.*

King of Kings

Grace and peace to you from. . .Jesus Christ,
who is the faithful witness, the firstborn from
the dead, and the ruler of the kings of the earth.

REVELATION 1:4–5 NIV

Jesus is King. He rules the kings of the earth even as we wait for His return when He will permanently set up His kingdom (Revelation 19). We often think of Jesus as King only as we anticipate His coming reign, but He is still very much King today. He rules the powers of the earth with His sovereignty.

Currently, Satan is in strong opposition to Jesus' rule, and we see the epic battle of good versus evil unfold every day. No matter how badly world events decline or how strong and powerful evil becomes, you can be confident the King of Kings is ultimately in control. The world may not make sense, but you can trust Jesus' ways and timing and find safety and security in His sovereignty.

King Jesus, sometimes the world feels out of control,
but I know You are in total control. I choose to trust
You and find peace and safety under Your rule.

Our High Priest

*My friends, the blood of Jesus gives us courage to
enter the most holy place by a new way that leads to
life! And this way takes us through the curtain that is
Christ himself. We have a great high priest who is in
charge of God's house. So let's come near God with
pure hearts and a confidence that comes from having
faith. Let's keep our hearts pure, our consciences free
from evil, and our bodies washed with clean water.*

HEBREWS 10:19–22 CEV

In the Old Testament, God's physical presence dwelled
inside the temple in a section called the Most Holy Place. A
curtain separated the Most Holy Place from the Holy Place
(Exodus 26:33). Only the high priest was allowed in the Most
Holy Place—and only once a year on the Day of Atonement
(Leviticus 16). When Jesus died, the curtain in the temple
ripped in two (Matthew 27:51). We are no longer separated
from God's presence! You can confidently approach Him
about *anything*.

*Jesus, thank You for being my High Priest
so I can always be in Your presence.*

Treasure Hunt

"The kingdom of heaven is like treasure hidden in a field.
When a man found it, he hid it again, and then in his
joy went and sold all he had and bought that field."

MATTHEW 13:44 NIV

Jesus shared a powerful truth about the kingdom of heaven in this simple story. The truth of who Jesus is (John 3:16), what He's rescued us from (Luke 16:22–24), and what He offers us for eternity (1 Peter 1:3–5) is such a profound treasure that it should flood us with joy and cause us to voluntarily give up *everything* to possess it.

Jesus Christ and His kingdom are treasures of incomparable worth. He surpasses anything we could pursue in this world. Do you see Jesus as that treasure? Are you pursuing Him passionately above everything else? Or is He just kinda worth your time? If you just sorta dabble with Christian activities, you don't yet fully understand the treasure Jesus is and offers. Keep digging deeper until you find it!

Jesus, help me recognize the treasure You
are and value You enough that I'd give
up everything in a heartbeat for You.

What Do You Say?

When Jesus came to the region of Caesarea Philippi, he asked his disciples, "Who do people say the Son of Man is?" They replied, "Some say John the Baptist; others say Elijah; and still others, Jeremiah or one of the prophets." "But what about you?" he asked. "Who do you say I am?" Simon Peter answered, "You are the Messiah, the Son of the living God."

MATTHEW 16:13–16 NIV

This was a defining moment for the disciples. They had witnessed Jesus' miracles. Heard His teaching. Followed Him for some time now. Through a series of questions, Jesus led them to a moment of clarity when they professed their faith in Him for the first time.

People today offer the same answers about Jesus. Many declare that Jesus was a great teacher, or a prophet, or an influential religious man who encouraged peace and love. Or they simply say He was a good person. But the piercing question is "Who do you say Jesus is?" Have you experienced that life-defining realization and declaration like the disciples?

Lord, I know this is the most important question I will ever answer. I say You are. . . .

Praise Him!

*My heart is confident in you, O God; my heart is
confident. No wonder I can sing your praises! . . . I will
thank you, Lord, among all the people. I will sing your
praises among the nations. For your unfailing love
is as high as the heavens. Your faithfulness reaches
to the clouds. Be exalted, O God, above the highest
heavens. May your glory shine over all the earth.*

PSALM 57:7, 9–11 NLT

Overwhelmed with gratefulness to answered prayer (Psalm
57:6), David burst out with praise to God. Once again, God had
proven Himself steady, faithful, and true. David's confidence
in the Lord strengthened and increased, and he couldn't
help but worship the amazing God who loves so constantly
and faithfully.

When has God answered your prayers in an overwhelming
way? How did those moments build your confidence in Him?
How can remembering those moments build your confidence
now? Take a moment to reflect on the goodness of the Lord
and what He's done in your life. Then burst into your own
words of worship and praise.

*Lord, I praise You! You have been so faithful
to me! My heart is confident in You.*

New Identity

*This means that anyone who belongs to
Christ has become a new person. The old
life is gone; a new life has begun!*

2 CORINTHIANS 5:17 NLT

When we ask Jesus to forgive our sins and we surrender our lives to Him, we begin a new life. God cleanses us and restores us spiritually. We go from spiritually dead in our sins to spiritually resurrected and alive! We are a new person—and we have a new identity.

Our old identities have lived with us so long they can feel permanently attached to us. Our old identities speak lies and destroy our confidence: "I don't belong. I'm unlovable. I'm not good enough." But you have a new identity in Christ! Recognizing and understanding who you are in Christ will give you the confidence and security you need.

What old identity still creeps around your thoughts? What do you believe about yourself—and does that match with who Christ says you are? That old life has gone! Step into your new identity, and let the truth of who you are in Christ give you assurance and freedom!

*Lord, help me understand who I am
in You and embrace my new identity.*

Child of God

But to all who believed him and accepted him,
he gave the right to become children of God.

JOHN 1:12 NLT

You are a child of God. If you have confessed your sins and accepted Jesus' gift of salvation, you are God's daughter! He's adopted you into His family! "I will be your Father, and you will be my sons and daughters, says the LORD Almighty" (2 Corinthians 6:18 NLT). And since we are His daughters, God has made us His heirs (Galatians 4:7). We will inherit His kingdom (James 2:5), and we have assurance that we will inherit eternal life (Titus 3:7).

You have a place in God's family. You are wanted and accepted. You have purpose and value. The world constantly tells you that you are not enough, but in God's sight, you are everything. Hold your head high and face today with confidence. You're a daughter of the King!

Father, thank You for adopting me into Your family.
When the world tries to tell me I'm worthless,
help me remember how much You love me and
how much value I have in Your eyes.

Called by Name

*"Do not be afraid, for I have ransomed you.
I have called you by name; you are mine."*

Isaiah 43:1 NLT

God knows your name. Who's your favorite celeb? Imagine going to an event where they'll be. You're jammed into the tight crowd of fans, but the celeb turns, looks straight at you, and calls your name. How floored would you be that this celebrity *knows your name*?!

God, the Creator and Sustainer of the universe, knows *your* name. He's called you out of the masses of humanity and claimed you as His own. He paid your ransom for sin, and you are His. God is not some "Man Upstairs" who's so busy running the world that He doesn't notice you or care about you. He is a strong Father who unconditionally loves you. He sees you and knows your name. He will do anything to save you and protect you.

How does the truth that God claims you give you reassurance today?

*God, I'm so humbled that You've ransomed me
and called me by name. I have incredible worth
and value to You. May this truth sink deep into
my heart and give me confidence today.*

Unconditionally Loved

*I am sure that nothing can separate us from
God's love—not life or death, not angels or spirits,
not the present or the future, and not powers above
or powers below. Nothing in all creation can separate
us from God's love for us in Christ Jesus our Lord!*

ROMANS 8:38-39 CEV

You are loved. Unconditionally. Completely. Just as you are.
Do you truly believe that? Nothing you've done in the
past—or will do in the future—changes God's love for you.
Nothing that's been done to you changes God's love for
you. None of your failures and flaws change God's love for
you. He *loves* you. Take a minute to really soak in the enormity
of this love. Let love comfort you, heal broken places inside
you, and give you confidence as you face this day.

*Loving Father, thank You for Your amazing love! You
always accept me, always have time for me, always
want to be with me, and always love me—no matter
what. Help me truly grasp how much You love me. May
Your love heal my broken and hurting places inside.*

Fully Forgiven

*He has removed our sins as far
from us as the east is from the west.*

PSALM 103:12 NLT

You are forgiven. God's forgiveness is different than human forgiveness. In our human nature, we might forgive, but we don't forget. God? His forgiveness deletes our sin forever. East and west never intersect. If you head east, you can continue heading east forever. If you head west, you can travel west forever. That's how far God has removed your sin: it's forever separated from you.

Not only has God completely removed your sin, but He "remembers your sins no more" (Isaiah 43:25 NIV). So when you confess and ask God to forgive your sins, they're gone! Shame has no place in your life. Guilt has no place in your life. God doesn't remember your sin, so you can forget about it too. Live free and confident in the amazing gift of forgiveness God gives us!

*Amazing Father, Your gift of forgiveness is astounding.
Thank You for forgiving me. Help me let go of guilt
and shame and live confidently in Your forgiveness.*

Redeemed

"I have swept away your offenses like a cloud,
your sins like the morning mist. Return
to me, for I have redeemed you."

ISAIAH 44:22 NIV

You are redeemed. Like Adam and Eve's sin did, our sin cast us out of God's presence forever. We lived cursed and condemned. But when Jesus hung on the cross, He took that curse upon Himself (Galatians 3:13). His sacrificial death on our behalf purchased our freedom and granted us forgiveness (Colossians 1:14). We can return to God's presence! We no longer must be separated from Him.

Is shame forcing you away from God? Does guilt cause you to keep God at a distance? You are *redeemed*, girl! Your guilt and shame are gone. Your sins have been paid for. Return to the loving arms of your Father. He loves you. He forgives you. He wants you to come home to Him.

Jesus, I am overwhelmed at the price You paid
to redeem me. The depth of Your love for me is
hard to grasp. Redeem my past mistakes, and use
what brings me shame to bring You glory.

Chosen

"I no longer call you slaves, because a master doesn't confide in his slaves. Now you are my friends, since I have told you everything the Father told me. You didn't choose me. I chose you."

JOHN 15:15–16 NLT

You are chosen. God calls you His friend when you are obedient to Him (John 15:14). Jesus desires to confide in you and reveal to you what the Father reveals to Him. He has written your name on the palms of His hands as a sign that He will never forget you (Isaiah 49:15–16). Even if your father and mother abandon you, the Lord will gladly take you in (Psalm 27:10). He takes great delight in you and rejoices over you with singing (Zephaniah 3:17). The infinite, almighty Creator of the universe chose *you* to be His friend! The world may reject you, but you can overcome any rejection with the confidence of God's love and friendship.

Jesus, I'm so blown away that You would choose me to be Your friend. When I feel rejected and left out, help me remember how much I'm truly loved.

Never Alone

Where could I go to escape from your Spirit or
from your sight? If I were to climb up to the highest
heavens, you would be there. If I were to dig down
to the world of the dead you would also be there. . . .
Or suppose I said, "I'll hide in the dark until night
comes to cover me over." But you see in the dark
because daylight and dark are all the same to you.

PSALM 139:7–8, 11–12 CEV

You are never alone. God's presence is with you—all the time,
everywhere. You may feel broken, abandoned, used, or unloved,
but here's the truth: nothing you've done or experienced will
ever change God's love for you. His presence stays with you
wherever you try to hide. Even if you're in a rebellious state,
God doesn't abandon you and longs for your return (Luke
15:11–31). God may not be pleased with your behavior, but
God's displeasure in disobedience is separate from His love
for you. His love never wavers. His presence never disappears.
His arms are always open.

Lord, You see me, and You never
leave me, even when I run from You.

Securely Held

*"I am God now and forever. No one can
snatch you from me or stand in my way."*

ISAIAH 43:13 CEV

You are securely held. God is your ultimate bodyguard. No power even remotely matches His. He fights for you against Satan's lies and schemes. His love chases you when you run away from Him. He lights up the shadows when you're surrounded by darkness. His power kicks down all the barriers standing in the way of where He wants you to go. He protects you and guards your heart and mind with peace when you're flooded with fear.

Do you see the fierce way He loves and protects you? Do you see the awesomeness of His incomparable power? Do you see the security and safety you have in His care? Rest in confidence and peace that you have Someone in your corner who is always fighting for you, shielding you, and watching over you. God's got you, and He'll never let go!

*God, Your love for me is overwhelming.
Thank You for claiming me, fiercely
guarding me, and never letting me go!*

Intrinsic Value

God created humanity in God's own image,
in the divine image God created them,
male and female God created them.

GENESIS 1:27 CEB

You have value. But that value isn't because of how you look or because you belong to the right teams or clubs or because you're smart. Strip away all your talents and abilities, and you still have value. Why? Because you're made in the image of God. Of everything God created, He only stamped His divine image on humans. That means He's placed something intrinsic in you that reflects who He is.

Imagine a diamond ring falls to the ground and gets trampled on. Dirty and dented, does it still have the same value? Of course! The world tries to make you feel like you don't have value unless you dress, behave, and believe a certain way. People will mistreat you, use you, and bully you. But no matter how dirty and dented you may feel, your value has never changed. How does that assurance alter how you see yourself?

God, so often I feel like my value is in my
looks or abilities. But my value comes
from You and can't be lost or changed.

Planned for a Purpose

You are the one who put me together inside my mother's body, and I praise you because of the wonderful way you created me. . . . Nothing about me is hidden from you! I was secretly woven together out of human sight, but with your own eyes you saw my body being formed. Even before I was born, you had written in your book everything about me.

PSALM 139:13–16 CEV

You are created for a purpose. Some of us can say we were born "on accident"—our parents weren't trying to get pregnant. But no one can say God created us "on accident." Your existence was purposeful and planned by our amazing Creator. He lovingly formed you in your mother's womb because He knew this world needed you.

You play a specific role that can only be filled by you. You have a purpose. Whether your parents "planned" you or not, you were most definitely planned and wanted by the Father!

Lord, I am no accident to You. I have value and purpose in Your eyes. Please guide me and show me the plans and purposes You intend for me.

Place to Belong

Through Christ, God has given us the privilege and authority as apostles to tell Gentiles everywhere what God has done for them, so that they will believe and obey him, bringing glory to his name. And you are included among those Gentiles who have been called to belong to Jesus Christ.

ROMANS 1:5-6 NLT

You belong to Jesus. The question of where we belong often plagues us. You may feel like you don't really belong at school. You have friends, but you don't have a close circle of friends. You're always on the fringe, never fully part of a group. Not feeling accepted can really feed our insecurity and shake our confidence. When you find yourself searching for a place to belong, repeat this truth to yourself: "I belong to Jesus."

Jesus accepts you. He claims you as His own. He warmly welcomes you into His circle of friends. Spend time with Him each day and let His love wrap around you like a cozy blanket, giving you the security and confidence you need.

Jesus, help me always remember I belong to You. Help me also find a healthy place to belong here.

God's Masterpiece

For we are God's masterpiece.
EPHESIANS 2:10 NLT

You are God's masterpiece. Merriam-Webster defines *masterpiece* as "a work done with extraordinary skill" and "a supreme intellectual or artistic achievement." God created you with extraordinary skill, carefully choosing just the right shade of your skin, eyes, and hair. No one on earth looks exactly the same (even twins are slightly different!).

You are God's masterpiece because there is no one else like you—and there never will be. Don't throw shade on God's supreme artistic achievement by hating certain parts of your body. "My thighs are so big." "I hate my hair." "My nose is so embarrassing!" God lovingly crafted each part of you. Don't insult Him by thinking ugly thoughts about yourself—or others. The enemy wants to destroy your beauty by making you discontented and by making you believe lies about how you look. Stand confident in your identity as God's masterpiece. You are beautiful!

Wow, God, it's mind-blowing to consider the billions and billions of masterpieces You've made! And I'm one of them. Help me see myself through Your eyes and appreciate Your skill instead of hating certain parts of my body.

Holy and Perfect

Even before he made the world,
God loved us and chose us in Christ
to be holy and without fault in his eyes.

EPHESIANS 1:4 NLT

You are without fault in God's eyes. God is all-knowing. He knew before He created the world how this human project was gonna go down—that we'd mess it up and He would have to send Jesus to fix it. And He loved us so much—He wanted a relationship with us so badly—He chose to create the world anyway.

When we repent and accept Jesus' sacrifice on the cross on our behalf, God gives us a new identity. We're no longer guilty sinners deserving of punishment. In Christ, we are holy and without fault in His eyes! So that shame you feel? He doesn't see it! The guilt you carry? It's gone! It's *gone.* You are holy, blameless, forgiven, *free.* Stand tall, girl! Shed that shame and guilt that weighs you down and walk confidently in your identity as a girl clean and holy!

God, I look in the mirror every day and find
so much fault with myself. But You don't!
You see me as perfect and holy.

Complete Victory

*No, in all these things we have complete
victory through him who loved us!*

ROMANS 8:37 GNT

You have complete victory through Jesus! Wow, what a powerful promise! What sins do you feel trapped under, like you can never get free? "It's impossible," you say. "I'll never be able to stop. . ." Cutting? Having sex? Starving yourself to stay skinny? Pleasing people for approval? Worrying? Whatever your struggle, you can have complete victory through Jesus!

"I've tried to stop!" you say. "My weakness keeps pulling me back. This is just who I am." BIG FAT LIE!!! Sure, the battle for freedom includes setbacks, but a failure does not define who you are. You are a victor! Get up and battle again until you gain complete freedom. Gather a group of trusted friends who know your struggle and can support you. You may need counseling to identify root issues that cause your behavior.

No sin has greater power than Jesus, so don't give sin ultimate power in your life. You're not a *victim of*. Confidence chooses to say, "I'm a *victor over!*" Sin cannot defeat you. In Christ you have *complete victory!*

Jesus, I claim victory over. . . .

Shove Off!

Throw off your old sinful nature and your former way of life, which is corrupted by lust and deception. Instead, let the Spirit renew your thoughts and attitudes. Put on your new nature, created to be like God—truly righteous and holy.

EPHESIANS 4:22-24 NLT

Our old sinful nature loves to deceive us. It corrupts our minds with lies like, "I can't do it. I'm not good enough." Throw off that thought as soon as it hits your brain! Let the Spirit renew your mind. Put on your new nature. Speak truth to yourself about who you are in Christ: "I can do all things through Christ, because he gives me strength" (Philippians 4:13 NCV).

The old sinful nature gets insecure and thinks, "No one really likes me. I'm unloved." Shove that thought into the trash! Think your new thought: The Lord says, "I have loved you with a love that lasts forever" (Jeremiah 31:3 CEB).

Your old nature wants to steal your confidence. Choose to throw off those deceitful, destructive thoughts and attitudes, and renew your mind with truth!

Spirit, help me toss those old attitudes and renew my thoughts with truth.

Let Him Lead

*"Follow me," Jesus said to him, and Levi
got up, left everything and followed him.*

LUKE 5:27-28 NIV

All the female needs to know in ballroom dancing is the basic step. That's it! Your partner does all the work. If you can follow his signals, he'll guide you across the floor like you're a pro. But that's the tricky part for us girls—it's not always easy to follow! Lack of trust makes us stiff. We take control by resisting our partner's cues and not moving where he wants us to go. We don't glide across the floor. Instead, the dance becomes a battle.

Jesus has called us to follow Him. Do you let Him lead? Or do you fight for control and push to move in a certain direction? Be confident in your Partner, and relax into the dance! When we let go of fear and control and move in trust with Jesus, following Him becomes smooth, peaceful, and beautiful.

*Jesus, trusting You feels scary sometimes.
Build my confidence in You so I know You won't
let me trip and fall. Help me let go of control
and follow You wherever You lead.*

Wrangling Resentment

But the snake said to the woman, "You will not die. God knows that if you eat the fruit from that tree, you will learn about good and evil and you will be like God!"

GENESIS 3:4-5 NCV

That sting of jealousy—you know exactly what it feels like. She has it *all*, and it's Just. Not. Fair. Jealousy, if not checked, easily transforms into resentment. You start thinking God loves *her* and not you. God is blessing *him* and not you. Really what it boils down to is this: You think God is not fair. He doesn't love you.

That's how Satan tricked Eve too. He twisted God's command so Eve felt like God was withholding something from her. Instead of seeing God's command as her protection, Eve grew resentful. "Why is God keeping this from me? He's not loving! I should have this so I can be wise." Her resentment gave birth to sin. Where is your jealousy leading you?

Loving Father, forgive me for resenting You. You only want what's best for me. Help me recognize the lies about You and trust Your ways are right.

Worrywart

"I tell you not to worry about your life. Don't worry about having something to eat, drink, or wear. Isn't life more than food or clothing? Look at the birds in the sky! They don't plant or harvest. They don't even store grain in barns. Yet your Father in heaven takes care of them. Aren't you worth much more than birds? Can worry make you live longer?"
MATTHEW 6:25-27 CEV

Life is full of worries. *Do I look pretty enough? Am I going to do well on my test? Will my parents divorce? Will I ever marry?* Thoughts and fears about the future can be overwhelming. *College? Career? I have no idea! How am I supposed to know?* But Jesus tells us to take a deep breath and just stop—stop the worry, stop the racing thoughts, stop focusing on the problem and put your eyes on Him. Let it go. He's got this.

Lord, I give You all my worries—from the little things to the big things. You will provide. Fill me with Your peace and joy as I let go and trust You.

Fashion Focused

"Has anyone by fussing in front of the mirror ever gotten taller by so much as an inch? All this time and money wasted on fashion—do you think it makes that much difference? Instead of looking at the fashions, walk out into the fields and look at the wildflowers. They never primp or shop, but have you ever seen color and design quite like it? . . . If God gives such attention to the appearance of wildflowers—most of which are never even seen—don't you think he'll attend to you, take pride in you, do his best for you?"

MATTHEW 6:27-30 MSG

God is a master artist—painting sunsets, sculpting canyons, and forming *you*. Of everything God has created, *you* are God's masterpiece—just as you are, without makeup, curling irons, and trendy clothes. Do you see yourself that way? Enjoying fashion is okay, but God sees past the clothes to who He made you to be. Don't nitpick all your imperfections, but celebrate the unique person you are.

Father, thank You for making me me. Help me not to focus on things that don't matter. Help me be confident in the way You shaped me.

Overconfidence

Trust in the LORD with all your heart. Never rely on what you think you know. . . . Never let yourself think that you are wiser than you are.

PROVERBS 3:5, 7 GNT

You're a teenager now! You have *all* the answers, right? You don't need your parents telling you what to do—you've got it figured out. Every teenager on the planet is tempted to think that. As we grow in independence, it's natural to start pushing away from our parents. But there's wisdom in not being overconfident in yourself. Your parents and other adults have a lot more experience than you, and the lessons they share are worth paying attention to.

Overconfidence makes you believe you are strong, capable, and brave and don't need anyone's help. Overconfidence is simply pride, and that's a sin. True confidence means having the wisdom and humility to place your trust where it belongs—first, in Jesus, and also in other trustworthy adults who can help guide you. How are you overconfident? How is God prompting you to show humility and true confidence?

Lord, forgive me for my pride. Help me be humble and teachable and listen to the wisdom of others.

Shine, Girl!

"You are like light for the whole world. . . . No one lights a lamp and puts it under a bowl; instead it is put on the lampstand, where it gives light for everyone in the house. In the same way your light must shine before people, so that they will see the good things you do and praise your Father in heaven."

MATTHEW 5:14-16 GNT

Peer pressure is real. You want to fit in and be accepted. No one likes to stand out and set themselves up for teasing and bullying. Yet following Jesus means going against the flow. You're going to stand out—and you're supposed to. But sometimes we like to slip that bowl over our light and kinda hide it a bit, you know? Here's the thing: darkness *needs* the light. Your school, your social circle, your community *needs* the light you have. Push back against the darkness and let your light shine!

Lord, forgive me for being afraid sometimes to let my light shine. Give me courage and boldness to stand for You so others can see You and find You.

Girl of Grace

[Love] is not easily angered,
it keeps no record of wrongs.

1 CORINTHIANS 13:5 NIV

The awkward friendship dance can really hit your insecurities. Are we friends. . .or not? You might be texting up a frenzy with someone, then all of a sudden it's total silence. You start questioning yourself. *Did I do something wrong? Why doesn't she like me? What's wrong with me?*

Navigating relationships can be *so* tricky, not to mention emotionally exhausting. Kick your insecurities to the curb and stay confident in yourself by *choosing* not to be easily angered. Was that supposed to be a slight? Choose to overlook it and not let it bother you. Feeling the cold shoulder? Choose not to take it personally. Maybe she's just really busy. Even if you *know* something was meant as a dig, you can choose to brush it off. By showing grace instead of taking offense, your friendships will remain strong—and you'll feel a lot more secure too!

Lord, help me not to read into things and take offense where maybe it wasn't intended. Help me show grace to my friends, just as You show grace to me.

You Do You

*In those days Israel had no king; all the people
did whatever seemed right in their own eyes.*

JUDGES 21:25 NLT

Our culture has abandoned truth. The world tells us that
biological sex doesn't matter—you can choose whatever gender
(or nongender) you want to be. You can choose whatever
gender you're sexually attracted to—or both! These and many
other lies are accepted—even celebrated. Diving into this issue
can be very complex and should be treated carefully and
lovingly. Yet we also cannot abandon God's truth.

Our culture has rejected Jesus as King (Romans 1:21-32).
But we have the Spirit of Truth who guides us (John 16:13).
Speaking the truth is not popular—it didn't win Jesus any
points with the crowd either. But Jesus had the courage to
love people *and* stand for truth at the same time. How do you
need to follow Jesus' example?

*Spirit of Truth, please guide me in what is right.
King Jesus, please give me courage to stand
for truth. Help me to find the balance of loving
others, yet not compromising my beliefs.*

Good or Bad Influence?

"It will be terrible for people who cause even one of my little followers to sin. Those people would be better off thrown into the deepest part of the ocean with a heavy stone tied around their necks!"

MATTHEW 18:6 CEV

Loving parents protect their children from danger and harm. God, as our loving Father, fiercely guards His children as well. Causing another believer to sin is a very serious offense to God. Your words and actions matter. If your gossip leads another Christian to gossip, God is greatly displeased. If your prejudice causes you to exclude someone deemed "lesser" and your Christian friends follow your example, God will hold you accountable.

You can be certain your influence on others matters a great deal to God. He promises sobering consequences if our behavior leads another Christian to stumble into sin. Carefully examine your life. Are your words honoring Jesus? Would your actions make Jesus proud?

God, thank You for this reminder that my influence is a serious matter. Show me how I haven't been honoring You. Help me lead people toward You and not away from You.

Listen Up!

While Peter was talking, a bright cloud covered them.
A voice came from the cloud and said, "This is my Son,
whom I love, and I am very pleased with him. Listen to him!"
MATTHEW 17:5 NCV

"Listen to me!" How many times a week do you hear this from your parents? What does your mom *really* mean when she says that? She's not saying to mindlessly hear what she says and then forget—that's why you get in trouble! She means *understand* what she's saying and *obey*.

God the Father audibly commanded Peter, James, and John to truly listen to Jesus—to not just hear what He says, but to seek to understand with a willingness to respond. God's command still echoes to us today: "Do not merely listen to the word, and so deceive yourselves. Do what it says" (James 1:22 NIV). How well do you listen to Jesus? When you read the Bible, are you seeking to understand what it says and obey its commands?

Jesus, help me truly listen to You—not just
mindlessly read my Bible or halfheartedly
listen at church. Help me understand Your
message and be willing to obey it.

Know It, Speak It!

*Jesus answered, "The Scriptures say:
'No one can live only on food. People
need every word that God has spoken.'"*

MATTHEW 4:4 CEV

Jesus was alone, hot, and HANGRY! He'd been fasting in the desert for forty days, and He was at the lowest of lows. Which is right when the enemy likes to attack. Satan came along and started tempting Jesus, but Jesus knew how to fight. With every temptation, Jesus quoted scripture and didn't let Satan twist God's commands.

How well do you know your Bible? We can stand confidently when we are strong in God's Word. How much scripture is hidden in your heart? The more you feed your soul with God's truth, the more you'll recognize Satan's lies and tricks. And when you're feeling low and vulnerable, you'll have the weapons to fight against temptation. Find a scripture that's meaningful to you, and start memorizing it today!

*Jesus, please help me know and memorize
Your Word so I can stand confidently
against the schemes of the enemy.*

Armor of God

Let the mighty strength of the Lord make you strong. Put on all the armor that God gives, so you can defend yourself against the devil's tricks. We are not fighting against humans. We are fighting against forces and authorities and against rulers of darkness and powers in the spiritual world. So put on all the armor that God gives. Then when that evil day comes, you will be able to defend yourself. And when the battle is over, you will still be standing firm.

EPHESIANS 6:10–13 CEV

A spiritual battle rages around you. Good news: God has already provided all the armor we need to survive this war— we just need to put it on! Bad news: without activating this armor, we're easy targets for Satan. Good news: we're not playing offense; we're only playing defense. Bad news: we can't let our guard down; we must always be prepared to fight. Great news: Christ already won the victory! Now we must hold that territory. Stand firm!

*Thank You, Lord, for equipping me for battle.
Help me stand firm and not let Satan push me around.
May Your mighty strength fill me and make me strong.*

Belt of Truth

*So stand strong, with the belt of
truth tied around your waist. . . .*

 EPHESIANS 6:14 NCV

Belts keep our clothing in place. In the same way, God's armor hinges on truth. Without truth and trustworthiness, the other armor can't stay in place. We can't stand against the enemy if we're able to be deceived. We must internalize God's truth so we can recognize the enemy's lies. Do you hear Satan whisper that you're not good enough? Do sly thoughts enter your mind that no one really likes you? That you're a screwup? That God doesn't really care? Those are all lies straight from the pit of hell. Hold your ground! Don't let the enemy invade your thoughts and chip away at your relationship with God and others. Saturate yourself with God's Word and confidently stand against the enemy's deceit.

*Lord, please reveal to me the lies I've accepted
about myself and about You. In the name of Jesus,
I rebuke those lies! Help me replace the lies with
Your truth so I can stand strong and not give
the enemy any kind of foothold in my life.*

Breastplate of Righteousness

*Stand firm then. . .with the breastplate
of righteousness in place.*

EPHESIANS 6:14 NIV

"Righteousness" is "right living." Paul wrote, "Do not let any part of your body become an instrument of evil to serve sin. Instead, give yourselves completely to God, for you were dead, but now you have new life. So use your whole body as an instrument to do what is right for the glory of God" (Romans 6:13 NLT).

Is your tongue glorifying God with the words you say? Are your eyes glorifying God with the things you watch and read? Are your ears glorifying God with the things you listen to? Righteous living protects our hearts from the attacks of the enemy. When we choose not to put on our breastplate of righteousness—when we choose not to "live rightly" and follow God's ways—we become vulnerable to sin. Evaluate all the areas of your life. How do you need to start living right?

*Lord, please forgive me for the ways I have
not lived rightly before You. Help me wear
the breastplate of righteousness so I can
protect myself from temptations to sin.*

Shoes of Peace

*For shoes, put on the peace that comes from the
Good News so that you will be fully prepared.*

EPHESIANS 6:15 NLT

We can confidently stand against the enemy when our feet are
firmly grounded in the peace that comes from Jesus. He said,
"Peace I leave with you; my peace I give you. I do not give to
you as the world gives. Do not let your hearts be troubled and
do not be afraid" (John 14:27 NIV). If we do not stand firmly
rooted in God's peace, then fear, anxiety, worry, and doubt
can overwhelm us. Suddenly we're unsure, then we feel like
we're standing on shaky ground.

Do not give the enemy a foothold in your life by stripping
away your peace. What unsettles you today? What worries
run through your mind? Bring each of those cares before
God in prayer and ask Him to fill you with His peace.

*Prince of Peace, I come before You now with all my
worries and all my fears. I trust in Your sovereign
control. Fill me with Your peace so I am protected from
the evil assaults of worry, doubt, fear, and anxiety.*

Shield of Faith

*At all times carry faith as a shield; for with it you will be
able to put out all the burning arrows shot by the Evil One.*

EPHESIANS 6:16 GNT

In this ongoing spiritual battle, we are to "be alert, be on
watch! Your enemy, the Devil, roams around like a roaring
lion, looking for someone to devour. Be firm in your faith and
resist him" (1 Peter 5:8–9 GNT). Carrying a shield of faith—
a determined resolve to trust Jesus—helps us stand firm
against the devil and resist his schemes. He shoots burning arrows of doubt straight at you—doubts about God's love,
goodness, trustworthiness, and faithfulness. He also tries
to shoot arrows of shame at you—thoughts that you aren't
good enough, worthy enough, faithful enough. Block those
arrows with your shield of faith! Stand firm on God's truth—
what's true about Him and about who you are in Christ.

What burning arrows are targeting you today? What
verses can you memorize and repeat to shield yourself
in faith?

*Lord, strengthen my faith so I can stand firm
and resist the devil. Show me verses I need
to memorize to block Satan's arrows.*

Helmet of Salvation

Accept God's salvation as your helmet. . .
EPHESIANS 6:17 NCV

You cannot resist any attacks from the enemy without salvation. As sinners, we are condemned to die physically and spiritually—being forever separated from God (Romans 6:23). The free gift of God is eternal life through Jesus—but we must accept it (Romans 6:23; 5:16–17). Once you have received salvation from God, then confidently secure your helmet.

The enemy will try to condemn you, shame you, and haunt you with your previous sin. You can resist these attacks by sheltering in the safety of your salvation. "Now there is no condemnation for those who belong to Christ Jesus" (Romans 8:1 NLT). God said, "I have swept your sins away like a cloud. Come back to me; I am the one who saves you" (Isaiah 44:22 GNT). Don't let the enemy knock you out with condemnation. Put on your helmet and rest securely in your salvation.

*Lord, thank You for dying for me and gifting me
with salvation. Help me not to accept feelings of
condemnation and unworthiness, but to stand
firm in the righteousness You give me.*

Sword of the Spirit

Take the sword of the Spirit,
which is the word of God.
EPHESIANS 6:17 NCV

Every piece of armor Paul listed so far has been defensive—only aimed at protecting the believer. Until now. The final piece of spiritual armor is our one and only offensive weapon—the Word of God. We are not to go charging against Satan (Paul clearly stated that our goal in this battle is just to stay standing and hold our ground). But of all the pieces of armor, the sword of the Spirit is how we deal blows to the enemy as we defend our ground. Jesus Himself used God's Word to fend off Satan (Matthew 4:3-11). God's Word is powerful!

How are you feeling tempted or attacked today? What scriptures can you memorize and repeat aloud to help you fight off the enemy? (For help, flip through this devotional and highlight your favorites!)

Holy Father, I praise You for being so strong and
mighty. Your Word alone is powerful enough to
send the enemy packing. Help me memorize Your
Word and use it effectively when Satan attacks me.

Posture of Prayer

And pray in the Spirit on all occasions with all kinds of prayers and requests. With this in mind, be alert and always keep on praying for all the Lord's people.

EPHESIANS 6:18 NIV

So we've put on the full armor of God. Next Paul described the attitude and posture we should continually maintain. We need to be prayerful and alert at all times. Attacks are imminent, from a crafty and cunning enemy. God's power and wisdom are needed as we navigate this ongoing warfare. Paul emphasized this vital need to pray at all times and with persistence and intensity. A nuclear war cannot be won with bows and arrows. Likewise, spiritual battles cannot be won with human effort. Prayer is our access to God's power and also keeps us alert to the spiritual dangers around us.

Regularly examine your armor. Does any piece need attention or repair? As you stand defensively against the enemy, stay alert and in prayer so you can confidently shout, "Not today, Satan!"

Lord, please guide me with Your wisdom, warning me of spiritual dangers. I also pray for. . .

See Ya, Satan!

Submit yourselves, then, to God.
Resist the devil, and he will flee from you.

JAMES 4:7 NIV

Satan is your number one enemy in this life. If you're on God's team, then the devil is going to attack you. He wants to steal, kill, and destroy any of God's blessings in your life (John 10:10). Should we be afraid of Satan? No! God has defeated him, and he's not nearly as powerful as Jesus. Should we be aware of Satan and his fighting tactics? Yes. So wear your spiritual armor and take your stand against the enemy's schemes. You can have total confidence that as you wear your armor and submit to God, Satan will run away from you. He's no match for Jesus!

Examine your life. Where is the enemy attempting to steal, kill, and destroy? Is he stealing your joy? Attempting to destroy a relationship through miscommunication and division? Killing your confidence? Submit to God, and make that evil scumbag skedaddle!

Jesus, I submit myself to You. I choose to be on Your team and let You be the Captain. Help me recognize Satan's attacks and resist them.

Confidence Killer

*Pay careful attention to your own work, for then you
will get the satisfaction of a job well done, and you
won't need to compare yourself to anyone else. For
we are each responsible for our own conduct.*

GALATIANS 6:4–5 NLT

You wanna know the best way to have confidence? Stop comparing yourself to others. There will *always* be someone prettier than you, more fashionable than you, smarter than you, more athletic than you. . .and on and on and on. Stop trying to achieve some impossible standard. Put on blinders and just look at yourself. Are you doing the best *you* can do? Don't sell yourself short. If you know you can try harder, do it. If you can be proud of what you've accomplished because you gave it your absolute best, then that's enough.

Comparison is an automatic confidence killer. So when you're tempted to measure yourself against someone else, chuck that thought and be proud of who God made *you* to be!

*Lord, it's so easy to lose my confidence when
I'm comparing myself to others. Help me
do my best and be satisfied with that.*

Fear Factor

For God has not given us a spirit of fear and
timidity, but of power, love, and self discipline.
2 TIMOTHY 1:7 NLT

Fear. It's everywhere. Fear of getting sick. Fear of not being accepted. Fear of the future. The enemy uses fear to sideline us. Satan wants to cause such an interruption in our lives that we stop playing the game. Because what does fear do? It paralyzes us. We stop trusting God. We no longer do what God wants us to do because we're so afraid.

But that's not how God wants us to live! When we live in fear, we've taken our eyes off God and focused on the problem. We need to fix our eyes on Jesus and stay confident in who He is and His promises to us. You can walk in confidence, power, and love because you know God is sovereign, He is always with you, He is good and fair, and He loves you. When you are tempted to be afraid, remember: don't let your fear be bigger than your God!

Almighty Father, You alone are the most
powerful in the universe. Forgive me for
nurturing fear and not trusting You.

Power Up!

I also pray that you will understand the incredible greatness of God's power for us who believe him. This is the same mighty power that raised Christ from the dead and seated him in the place of honor at God's right hand in the heavenly realms.

EPHESIANS 1:19-20 NLT

The same power that raised Christ from the dead is in you. Let that sink in. The *same power* that *raised Christ from the dead* is in *YOU*! His power fills us with endurance, patience, and joy (Colossians 1:11). It turns our weakness into strength (2 Corinthians 12:9-10). It gives us boldness to share Jesus with our family members, friends, and strangers (Acts 1:8). His power frees us from sin (Romans 6:6).

How have you been living powerless when you could be powerful? How do you need to tap into God's power? Ask God to help you understand the incredible greatness of His power and how He wants you to live in that power today.

Mighty God, I cannot even begin to grasp the fullness of Your power that lives in me. Help me live in that power for the glory of Your name.

What's Your Score?

My brothers and sisters, think of the various tests you encounter as occasions for joy. After all, you know that the testing of your faith produces endurance. Let this endurance complete its work so that you may be fully mature, complete, and lacking in nothing.

JAMES 1:2–4 CEB

When life gets tough, how do you react? Do you moan and complain, becoming bitter at the injustice? Do you freak out, becoming a ball of stress and anxiety? Maybe you shut down and ignore the pain. Challenges reveal our weak spots. When we're under pressure, we gain a solid view of what we truly treasure and trust. Tests expose how much we need God and give us a chance to evaluate how well we're depending on Him—or where there's definite room for improvement.

So how do you score? What do the challenges in your life reveal about your faith?

Father, spiritual tests are not fun. But I'm thankful for them because they show me what's really inside. Help me to grow in my faith, to put my trust in You, and to continue growing into a more mature, confident woman.

False Confidence

"Not everyone who calls out to me, 'Lord! Lord!' will enter the Kingdom of Heaven. Only those who actually do the will of my Father in heaven will enter. On judgment day many will say to me, 'Lord! Lord! We prophesied in your name and cast out demons in your name and performed many miracles in your name.' But I will reply, 'I never knew you. Get away from me, you who break God's laws.'"

MATTHEW 7:21-23 NLT

Did you catch what Jesus said? He said *many* will come to Him expecting to enter the kingdom of heaven. But they have a false confidence. They missed what salvation is really about. It's not what you *do*, how much you *know*, or how *good* you are. It's about where you place your trust.

What is the will of the Father? That you believe Jesus is the Messiah and accept His sacrifice as payment for your sins (Romans 10:9-10). This decision should radically transform your life (Matthew 3:8; James 2:14-26). So. . .does Jesus know you? Who can you pray for that needs to know Him?

*Lord, show me what it means to
know You and trust in You.*

Not Ashamed!

For I am not the least bit embarrassed about the gospel. I won't shy away from it, because it is God's power to save every person who believes: first the Jew, and then the non-Jew.

ROMANS 1:16 VOICE

The Gospel is not popular. Have you noticed? Christians are being pushed more and more into the fringes of society. Sharing your beliefs may cause others to make fun of you, to bully you, or to outright shun you. It's so tempting to keep quiet—to just fit in and not make any waves.

That's not what God wants. We are to be girls who confidently live in the truth (Luke 9:26). We are not ashamed! The Gospel is powerful—it radically changes lives. It changed yours! Don't shy away from sharing it with others. And don't back down from the truth. People *need* the Gospel. God's power is behind you!

Lord, when I'm tempted to shy away from sharing Your truth, give me power and courage to stand for You. Holy Spirit, help me speak with boldness, and give me the words to say.

Counting the Cost

*Then a teacher of the law came to Jesus and said,
"Teacher, I will follow you any place you go." Jesus said to
him, "The foxes have holes to live in, and the birds have
nests, but the Son of Man has no place to rest his head."*

MATTHEW 8:19–20 NCV

Here comes a man ready to make his commitment to Jesus,
and Jesus is like, "Hold up. Are you sure? 'Cause following
Me ain't easy." There is a cost to following Jesus, and this is
not a commitment we make lightly. Jesus said life will be
hard. If people rejected Jesus Himself, they will reject His
followers too. Christians won't be welcome everywhere. We
must be willing to sacrifice *everything* to follow Him. He
requires our total surrender and unwavering trust. That's a
big ask, but He's worthy of it. How's your commitment to
Jesus? What is Jesus asking of you? Do you have the confidence in Him to be all in?

*Jesus, You ask a lot of me. But You also give me way
more than I deserve. Help me surrender everything
to You and follow You, especially when it's hard.*

Heart Evaluation

"Good people bring good things out of the good they stored in their hearts. But evil people bring evil things out of the evil they stored in their hearts. People speak the things that are in their hearts."

LUKE 6:45 NCV

What you say reveals what's in your heart. Pay attention to your words today. What do you say to your siblings? What do you say to your parents? What do you say to your friends? What do you say to people who are not your friends? What are you posting online? Are you saying evil things—negative words that harm and cause destruction? Or are you saying good things—positive encouragement that's life-giving? Are your words harsh and rebellious? Or loving and submissive?

Taking a genuine look at what's coming out of your heart gives you a good idea of your true spiritual health. What needs some work?

Ouch, God. I'm not as good as I thought. Forgive me, Jesus, and cleanse my heart. Help me work on memorizing Your Word and storing good things in my heart so that my words better reflect You.

True Greatness

"Instead, whoever wants to become great among you must be your servant, and whoever wants to be first must be your slave—just as the Son of Man did not come to be served, but to serve, and to give his life as a ransom for many."

MATTHEW 20:26-28 NIV

We naturally seek positions of power and popularity. We jockey to be first and the best. We selfishly put ourselves before others and desire honor, praise, and admiration. But in Jesus' kingdom, the servant exceeds the power player. That means if toilets need cleaned, we should be the first to volunteer. True greatness means we model Jesus in His humility, sacrifice, compassion, and service.

How do you jockey to be first? How do you expect to be served instead of serve? How can you model Jesus' servant leadership? How can you show compassion and service at school? How can you show humility and sacrifice at home?

Holy Spirit, work in my heart to help me overcome my selfishness. Help me put others before myself and willingly take humble positions and duties without complaining.

Childlike Faith

*Then he said, "I tell you the truth, you must change
and become like little children. Otherwise, you
will never enter the kingdom of heaven. The
greatest person in the kingdom of heaven is the
one who makes himself humble like this child."*

MATTHEW 18:3-4 NCV

The disciples argued with each other about which of them
would be the greatest in Jesus' kingdom (Luke 9:46). Jesus
gently corrected their worldly understanding of greatness
by illustrating true greatness in God's eyes. We must change
and become like toddlers. What?! But think about it. Toddlers
completely depend on their parents for everything—being fed
and dressed and having diapers changed. They humbly and
simply trust their parents to care and provide.

As we age and grow independent, we often take that
independence into our spiritual life. We think we can handle
it; we don't need God. But God wants us to keep that childlike
trust and dependence on Him. How has independence crept
into your relationship with God? How do you need more
childlike faith?

*Lord, help me live in total dependence and simple
trust that You will care and provide for me.*

Eternal Eyes

So we are always confident, even though we know that as long as we live in these bodies we are not at home with the Lord. For we live by believing and not by seeing. Yes, we are fully confident, and we would rather be away from these earthly bodies, for then we will be at home with the Lord.

2 CORINTHIANS 5:6–8 NLT

Why was Paul always confident? Because Paul knew we have eternal, heavenly bodies waiting for us, and we have the Holy Spirit as a guarantee that God will fulfill His promise (2 Corinthians 5:1–5). Our new bodies will never experience sickness, pain, injury, or death (Revelation 21:4). Imagine!

It's easy to let the things we see and feel drag us down. Sickness is miserable. Injuries can be very serious. The death of loved ones hurts. But we live by believing! It's not our temporary circumstances but our eternal destiny that gives us confidence. How can focusing on your eternal home with Jesus help you choose confidence today?

Lord, help me live with the confidence of an eternal perspective and not get so worked up about things that don't really matter.

Confident Prayer

This is the confidence that we have in our relationship with God: If we ask for anything in agreement with his will, he listens to us. If we know that he listens to whatever we ask, we know that we have received what we asked from him.

1 JOHN 5:14–15 CEB

We can pray with confidence because we know God listens and answers. However, God is not a genie in a bottle. "God, I want a new phone for my birthday!" Poof, wish granted! "God, I'd really like my sibling to be less annoying." Poof, answered! Prayer is not about giving God a laundry list of our requests and expecting them all to be granted. Prayer is about approaching God, seeking His will, and aligning our desires and expectations with His. Will He always answer those kinds of prayers? Absolutely! If you earnestly seek God for peace, comfort, or assurance, you can be confident He will always answer.

Lord, thank You for listening to me and answering me! Help me not to pray selfishly for things I want but to approach You with humility and to seek Your will.

Honor

*"This, then, is how you should pray: 'Our Father
in heaven: May your holy name be honored.'"*
MATTHEW 6:9 GNT

Now that we have free access to God—anytime, anywhere
(Hebrews 10:19-22)—Jesus gave a model of how we should
pray. God doesn't care if we say super-polished prayers that
sound impressive. Long, rambling prayers aren't an indication
of a strong spiritual life (Matthew 6:5-8). Rather, God wants
simple, genuine prayers that come from our hearts.

When we pray, we should begin by honoring God. God
is *holy*—set apart, worthy of complete devotion, and like
no other. Approach Him with the honor He deserves,
remembering who He is and all He has done. Spend time in
awe of this perfect, loving, and mighty God we serve, and let
your prayer start with praise and worship of our wonderful
King and Savior.

*Almighty God, You are worthy of my praise. You are
strong and powerful, creating galaxies with a spoken
word. Yet You are loving, calling me Your friend. You are
faithful, merciful, compassionate, and slow to anger.*

Submission

*"May your Kingdom come; may your will
be done on earth as it is in heaven."*

MATTHEW 6:10 GNT

After honoring God with our praise and worship, next we need to submit ourselves to Him. We acknowledge Him as King of our lives. In heaven God has unquestioned authority, and His rule is perfect. On earth we also need to bring ourselves under His perfect authority and lay down any rebellion or resentment we feel toward Him.

After praising Him, we must spend time doing heart work. How have you been fighting for your own way—with God, your parents, your siblings, or your friends? How have you been resisting the Holy Spirit's conviction? How are you mad at God for unfair circumstances? How are you tempted to handle things yourself without God's help? Take time to examine your thoughts and emotions. Confess any rebellion you're harboring, and stop trying to steer your own life.

*Father, You are the rightful King, on earth and in heaven.
I submit myself to You. May Your will be done in my life.*

Daily Dependence

"Give us today the food we need."
MATTHEW 6:11 GNT

Once we have properly worshipped our Creator and submitted our lives to Him, *then* we can bring our needs and requests before Him. So often we jump right into the needs part. "Hey, God, can You do this, this, and that? Thanks! Bye!" But Jesus is showing us that prayer is more than asking for help to solve our problems. Prayer is also how we show honor to God and realign our hearts to be in proper submission. Once our hearts are in the right place, then we are better able to present our requests to Him.

God faithfully provides for our physical and spiritual needs. We are to depend on Him each day to meet those needs. Do you trust Him to take care of you? How do you struggle to live in daily dependence on God?

*Good Father, You are a faithful Provider. I submit
my requests and wants to You. Please meet my
needs for this day as I depend on You.*

Cleansing Confession

*"Forgive us the wrongs we have done, as we
forgive the wrongs that others have done to us."*
MATTHEW 6:12 GNT

Our prayer time needs dedicated space for confession. God isn't Santa Claus who exists to hear our wishes and give us gifts. He is our holy and righteous Father who deserves the worship, submission, and respect we show by admitting to our general sinfulness and specific sins. We need to bring our dark sins into His light and allow Him to cleanse us.

The same grace we are given needs to be shown to others. Are you holding a grudge against your parents or siblings? Friends? Enemies? Are you allowing a petty offense to drive a wedge into a friendship? Maybe someone has truly hurt you in a big way. Is that hurt any bigger than what you've done to God? Ask God who you need to forgive and for His help to give the same grace you have received.

*Forgiving Father, I do not deserve Your grace.
But You freely give it. Please forgive me for
my sins, and help me forgive others.*

Deliver Us

*"And don't lead us into temptation,
but rescue us from the evil one."*
MATTHEW 6:13 CEB

Finally, we are to seek God's protection when we pray. We ask God to deliver us from our temptations and also from the schemes and traps of the enemy that lead us into sin and away from God. We must humbly recognize that we can't be strong enough, good enough, or faithful enough to rescue ourselves. We can't overpower sin on our own. We need a Savior, and we must rely on His strength, power, and perfection to save us. Our confidence is not in ourselves but in Him.

What temptations do you face today? How do you feel the pressure of the enemy to disobey God and go your own way? How do you need to admit you need God's help? Speak honestly with your Father and ask Him to rescue you—then watch expectantly for His deliverance.

*Mighty God, rescue me. Please protect me
today. Help me walk away from temptation
and shut it down. In my weakness, give me the
strength I need to stand against the enemy.*

Listening Prayer

"And the sheep listen to the voice of the shepherd.
He calls his own sheep by name and leads them out.
. . . They follow him because they know his voice."
JOHN 10:3-4 NCV

Prayer is a conversation. Jesus taught us how to pray, but there's still another component—listening. It's no fun to chat with a friend when she does *all* the talking. A good friend listens as well. Prayer is the same. I'm sure Jesus is *quite* familiar with your voice (we do a lot of talking when praying!). But are you familiar with His? Do you take time to stop talking, be still, and *listen* for what He longs to say to you?

Listening prayer takes practice. It's not easy to calm our minds and listen for His still, small voice. Maybe He'll prompt you to read a scripture that you need. Maybe He has some encouragement or conviction. Maybe He wants you to talk to someone or do something. The more you practice listening, the better you can recognize His voice.

Lord, still my mind and calm my racing thoughts.
What do You want to say to me today?

The Question

Two blind men were sitting by the roadside, and when
they heard that Jesus was going by, they shouted, "Lord,
Son of David, have mercy on us!" . . . Jesus stopped and
called them. "What do you want me to do for you?"
he asked. "Lord," they answered, "we want our sight."
Jesus had compassion on them and touched their eyes.
Immediately they received their sight and followed him.

MATTHEW 20:30, 32–34 NIV

Even though these blind men could not physically see, their
spiritual eyes were far from blind. They clearly recognized
Jesus for who He was—the Messiah. Jesus' question gently led
them from a general request for mercy to a statement of their
specific need. When they asked for sight, Jesus healed them.

Jesus asks us the same question: *"What do you want*
Me to do for you?" Many times we offer general prayers and
requests, but how would you answer this question right now?
What specific needs are you facing? How do you need spiritual
insight or understanding?

Lord, I need. . . . Please provide. Please touch me so I
can see and understand and follow where You lead.

Making Excuses

Another disciple said to him, "Lord, first let me go
and bury my father." But Jesus told him, "Follow
me, and let the dead bury their own dead."

MATTHEW 8:21-22 NIV

Whoa, Jesus! That's harsh! I thought we were supposed to honor
our parents. What's up with that? In Jewish culture, burials
took place the same day a person died. So most likely, this
man's father was still alive. He basically said to Jesus, "Now
isn't a great time. I want to follow You, but something else is
more important." Jesus responded with, "Spiritually dead
people are capable of performing a burial; they don't need
you. I want your loyalty. Will you put Me above everyone
and everything else?"

Don't misunderstand—Jesus isn't an uncaring and harsh
master. He healed Peter's mother-in-law when she was sick
(Matthew 8:14-15), and He promises to care for us (Matthew
6:25-33). But He doesn't want our excuses. How do you
justify your disobedience when you don't want to follow Jesus?
What's more important to you?

Lord, forgive me for making other things
more important than You. I surrender them
to You now and give You my loyalty.

Gimme, Gimme!

*Later, Matthew invited Jesus and his disciples to
his home as dinner guests, along with many tax
collectors and other disreputable sinners. But when
the Pharisees saw this, they asked his disciples,
"Why does your teacher eat with such scum?"*

MATTHEW 9:10–11 NLT

The Pharisees were jealous. Jesus spent all His time with
the "bad crowd." The Pharisees saw themselves as the
cool kids—the Goody Two-shoes who did everything right.
They had become so confident in their goodness that they
crossed the line into entitlement: "Why isn't Jesus hanging
out with *us* and showing *us* His favor and blessings? We're
the ones who deserve it!" We fall into the same trap when
we believe we *deserve* God's blessings because we've been
good, obedient, and faithful. But what do we truly deserve?
Death (Romans 6:23).

God delights in blessing us (Matthew 7:11), but our attitude
toward Him should always be one of humility and gratefulness.
Rewards and blessings are not our due. They are generous,
undeserved gifts from our loving Father.

*Lord, forgive me for feeling entitled to good things. I don't
deserve anything, and I'm truly grateful for Your grace.*

He's Got You!

"Two sparrows cost only a penny, but not even one of them can die without your Father's knowing it. God even knows how many hairs are on your head. So don't be afraid. You are worth much more than many sparrows."

MATTHEW 10:29–31 NCV

Jesus tasked His disciples with traveling in pairs through towns to be His witnesses (Matthew 10:1–8). However, Jesus warned that this would be no easy mission. Danger, rejection, and persecution awaited them (Matthew 10:16–23), but they could have confidence in Jesus' care and provision.

Do you even notice when a bird dies? God does! Could you even guess how many hairs are on your head? God knows exactly. If God pays so much attention to dead birds and numbered hairs, you can be confident He's intently watching over you. He might ask you to do hard or scary things, but He's right there with you every step of the way. When you're tempted to fear what's ahead, let the reminder of God's watchful care give you assurance.

God, You can be trusted. You are intently aware of everything, and I am never beyond Your care or protection.

Toss It!

Throw all your anxiety onto him,
because he cares about you.

1 PETER 5:7 CEB

Worry is the opposite of trust. Every time you worry, you are not putting your confidence in God. Can God handle whatever you're stressed about? Of course! He's big enough and strong enough to carry your anxiety for you. Jesus said, "Come to me, all you who are weary and burdened, and I will give you rest" (Matthew 11:28 NIV). Jesus takes our burdens for us so we can walk in freedom (Matthew 11:30).

Every time you worry, turn it into trust. Choose confidence by throwing your anxiety onto God and saying, "Jesus, I trust You." Let Him carry the burden for you so you can be at peace. What concerns are swirling in your mind today? Give them each to Jesus and choose to live in confidence and peace!

Jesus, I'm anxious about. . . . I throw these worries
onto You. Because You care about me, I trust
You to shoulder these fears for me so I can be at
peace. Remind me today each time I start to worry
again to stop and say, "Jesus, I trust You."

Flaky Friends

*Putting confidence in an unreliable person
in times of trouble is like chewing with a
broken tooth or walking on a lame foot.*

PROVERBS 25:19 NLT

Have you ever relied on someone to be there for you when
you really needed it, and they totally flaked? It's so frustrating!
And hurtful. Not everyone is worthy of your confidence. Who
you choose as friends is extremely important. Do you have
solid, reliable friends who give to you as much as you give
to them? Or are your friends Takers—they'll take everything
you give but they don't return the friendship favor? Closely
examine your friendships—how you treat your friends and
how they treat you. Lay off the unhealthy relationships and
let them go. Be thankful for and focus on the friends who love
you and stick around through thick and thin. If you need more
of those friends, ask Jesus to help you find them.

*Lord, give me wisdom in who I choose as friends.
Help me let go of unhealthy relationships and
nurture the friendships that are reliable and well
balanced. Help me be a good friend as well.*

The Right Touch

A man with a skin disease came, kneeled before him, and
said, "Lord, if you want, you can make me clean." Jesus
reached out his hand and touched him, saying, "I do want
to. Become clean." Instantly his skin disease was cleansed.

MATTHEW 8:2–3 CEB

According to Old Testament law, skin diseases made people
ritually unclean. This meant they were outcasts, unable to
mingle in society (Leviticus 13:45-46). No one could touch
them without becoming "unclean" too.

Did you catch what Jesus did? He *touched* the man. Jesus
only needed to speak for this man to be healed. He didn't have
to touch him. But Jesus saw his emotional and spiritual wounds.
Jesus healed him physically, and His touch also told this
man, "I see you. I see your pain from being cast out by society.
I accept you. I love you." Many times we pray for physical
needs, but God goes deeper and touches our emotional and
spiritual pain. How do you need God's touch today?

Lord, You see me—my physical, emotional,
and spiritual weaknesses. I need You,
and I want You. Please touch my life.

104

Honoring Others

*When you do things, do not let selfishness or
pride be your guide. Instead, be humble and give
more honor to others than to yourselves.*

PHILIPPIANS 2:3 NCV

The Trinity exists in this beautiful, mysterious relationship.
The Father delights in glorifying the Son (John 8:54). The Son
delights in glorifying the Father (John 17:1). And the Holy Spirit
delights in glorifying the Son, thereby glorifying the Father
(John 16:14). Each of them in love and humility reflects honor
to the others.

How often do you seek honor for yourself? Maybe jealousy
stabs when a sibling or friend receives a compliment and you
don't. Maybe when someone else is praised, you quickly think,
Well, what about me? Having confidence in who you are—that
you are accepted, loved, and given talents from God—allows
you to humbly honor others. Your security and identity in
Christ should erase any jealousy toward others and motivate
you to praise and honor them. Like the Trinity, we should
delight in glorifying others more than ourselves.

*Lord, help me not to be jealous when others are honored
and I'm not. Help me delight in honoring others, like You.*

Bible Quiz

I have hidden your word in my heart,
that I might not sin against you.
PSALM 119:11 NLT

How well do you know your Bible? Have you actually read the whole thing, from cover to cover? Now is a great time to start! The more you read, study, and memorize scripture, the less power Satan has to tempt you with sin and lies. *And* the more scripture you read, the more you'll hear the Holy Spirit speak to you. Score!

Feeling like we don't know the Bible very well can shake our confidence. What questions do you have about the Bible? How can you find the answers? Don't shy away from asking hard questions. Dig deep and learn. Wrestle. Pray. Ask God to meet you in your struggle. Build a strong foundation for your faith so when life's wrecking balls come to knock you down, you can stand with confidence on the solid Rock (Psalm 18:31).

God, there's so much I don't understand when I read Your Word, and honestly, some stuff is just plain weird. Meet me as I read, and help me find answers to my questions.

Walk the Talk

*Dear children, let's not merely say that we love each other;
let us show the truth by our actions. Our actions will
show that we belong to the truth, so we will be confident
when we stand before God. Even if we feel guilty, God
is greater than our feelings, and he knows everything.*

1 JOHN 3:18-20 NLT

If you say you are a Christian, do your actions prove it? Does your outward behavior reflect the inward reality of your personal relationship with Jesus? All of us sin and don't perfectly represent the truth of Jesus by our actions. But we should be in the process of transformation and becoming more and more like Him as our old, sinful habits die (Ephesians 4:20-24). Our changed desires and behavior give us confidence when we stand before God. We can clearly see His transforming work in our lives, and we know without question we are His children. How has God changed you? What sinful habit is God asking you to surrender now?

*Lord, continue working in my life, transforming
me from the inside out to be more like You.
Show me what habits need to go.*

God's Best

"I say this because I know what I am planning for you,"
says the LORD. "I have good plans for you, not plans
to hurt you. I will give you hope and a good future."

JEREMIAH 29:11 NCV

Here's a simple question: Do you believe God always wants what's best for you? Yes. So, if God is not giving you what you want, that means it's not the best thing for you right now. That can be a hard truth to accept. What we want seems like such a good thing! How could God withhold it? But God's thoughts are so much higher than ours (Isaiah 55:9). We can only see this moment, but God sees our whole future (1 Corinthians 13:12). If God is closing doors and telling you "no" or "wait," then you can be confident that what you desire is not what's best. Trust that something better is around the corner.

Lord, sometimes it's really hard to understand when You
deny me what I want. But I'm confident You know better
than I do, and I trust that Your plans for me are good.

Confident Peace

"But blessed are those who trust in the LORD and have made the LORD their hope and confidence. They are like trees planted along a riverbank, with roots that reach deep into the water. Such trees are not bothered by the heat or worried by long months of drought. Their leaves stay green, and they never stop producing fruit."

JEREMIAH 17:7-8 NLT

Planting all your confidence, hope, and trust in Jesus reaps a harvest of peace. No matter the circumstances that surround you, you can remain calm and confident because you know the Lord is in control, He is always with you, and He will protect and provide for you. The world around you may be drowning in anxiety, fear, hatred, and panic, but you can continuously produce the fruit of the Spirit and live in "love, joy, peace, patience, kindness, goodness, faithfulness, gentleness, and self-control" (Galatians 5:22-23 NLT).

How's your confidence today? Are you withering beneath the heat of the world or producing the fruit of the Spirit?

*Lord, I put my hope and trust in You.
I give You all my stress and trust You
to care for me. Today, I choose peace.*

Confident Failure

The way to please you is to be truly sorry deep in our hearts. This is the kind of sacrifice you won't refuse.

PSALM 51:17 CEV

When you have a royal mess-up, the best thing to do is face it with confidence. Own it and apologize for it. We naturally want to make excuses, justify our actions, or play the blame game. We'll go to great lengths to avoid the responsibility or label of being wrong. But that's not how God wants us to respond. He asks us to acknowledge our sin and be truly sorry. We must own it before Him and ask for His forgiveness. We also need to own it before others—with no excuses—and ask for forgiveness where needed.

The next time you back-talk your mom or disobey your dad, own your behavior and apologize to them. When you get caught in a lie, don't dig yourself deeper with more lies and justification. Admit the truth. God is pleased when you face your failures with confidence.

Lord, forgive me for. . . . Help me not to justify my actions or make excuses, but to apologize to others with confidence and humility.

Confident Knowledge

*Meanwhile, a Jew named Apollos, an eloquent speaker
who knew the Scriptures well, had arrived in Ephesus from
Alexandria in Egypt. He had been taught the way of the
Lord, and he taught others about Jesus with an enthusiastic
spirit and with accuracy. However, he knew only about
John's baptism. When Priscilla and Aquila heard him
preaching boldly in the synagogue, they took him aside
and explained the way of God even more accurately.*

ACTS 18:24–26 NLT

Although Apollos knew a lot, he had some knowledge gaps. Priscilla and Aquila took this gifted young man aside and mentored him so he could more thoroughly understand Jesus and the scriptures.

We all have knowledge gaps—even if we've been raised going to church! Like Apollos, don't be offended if someone wants to guide you to a better understanding of scripture. And like Priscilla and Aquila, respectfully and lovingly share your knowledge with others so they can have a better understanding of God.

How can you grow in your knowledge of the Bible? Who can you mentor so they can better understand God?

*Lord, deepen my understanding of scripture,
and show me who I can mentor to know You better.*

111

Confident Faith

*Now faith is confidence in what we hope for
and assurance about what we do not see.*

HEBREWS 11:1 NIV

Faith requires confidence because faith *is* confidence. Faith has total trust and certainty in God because of His nature, character, and promises. Faith is completely convinced in the reality of God, even though we cannot see Him. How confident is your faith?

Find your weak spots by identifying areas where you lack trust. Are you not totally sure about God's nature and who He is? Is there something about His character that's hard for you to accept or believe? What promises in the Bible do you have trouble trusting? Admit your doubts and uncertainties to God and ask Him to strengthen your trust and assurance in Him. He will always prove Himself faithful and trustworthy when we take small steps of faith toward Him.

*God, I want to have total trust and confidence in
You, but sometimes I'm just unsure. Please reveal
Yourself more and more to me so I can know You more
deeply and grow in my faith and certainty in You.*

Confident Hope

Don't put your confidence in powerful people;
there is no help for you there. . . . But joyful are
those who have the God of Israel as their helper,
whose hope is in the LORD their God.

PSALM 146:3, 5 NLT

People are looking for a Mr. Fix It. Someone to solve all our problems. Someone to swoop in and put right everything that's wrong in our neighborhoods, country, and world. While it is good and necessary to be involved in our schools and communities in civic matters, we cannot pin our hopes on a human to fix this world's messes. Our hope is not in powerful leaders. Our hope is in the God of Israel, who is infinitely more powerful than any human being.

Are you looking to a person to fix the problems around you? Are you putting your hope in someone other than God? Look to the Lord first, and keep your hope in Him. He alone will provide what you need.

Lord, so much is wrong in this world. No powerful
person can fix all the brokenness. My hope is in You.
Please restrain evil, fight for justice, and restore truth.

Confident Love

We know how much God loves us, and we have put our trust in his love. . . . And as we live in God, our love grows more perfect. So we will not be afraid on the day of judgment, but we can face him with confidence because we live like Jesus here in this world.

1 JOHN 4:16–17 NLT

Love changes everything. The more we understand how much God loves us, the more it transforms us. Love makes you patient, kind, humble, slow to anger, and forgiving (1 Corinthians 13:4-6). Love "always protects, always trusts, always hopes, always perseveres" (1 Corinthians 13:7 NIV). Jesus came in love, not to condemn and judge the world but to save it (John 3:17). God *loves* you! So much so that He willingly died for you. Soak in that love today. Let it heal you, restore you, and give you peace. Let God's love change you so you can confidently live like Jesus did—sharing His love with everyone.

Jesus, help me grasp how much You love me.
Let it heal my broken places. Let it change
me so I can share Your love with others.

Confident Trust

"The fire and wood are here," Isaac said, "but where is the lamb for the burnt offering?" Abraham answered, "God himself will provide the lamb for the burnt offering, my son." And the two of them went on together.

GENESIS 22:7-8 NIV

Abraham waited *twenty-five years* for God to fulfill His promise to give Abraham children through his wife Sarah. His confidence wavered during those years, and there were times when Abraham didn't fully trust God to do what He said. But sure enough, Isaac came along at the exact time God promised (Genesis 21:2).

Then God tested Abraham. He told Abraham to sacrifice Isaac as an offering to God (Genesis 22:1-2). Isaac was the guaranteed heir! Without Isaac, God's covenant couldn't be fulfilled. Abraham faced a choice: trust God with unwavering confidence even though it made *no* sense—or not. This time, Abraham had total confidence that God would keep His word. He took Isaac up the mountain, fully trusting that God would provide another sacrifice, which God did (Genesis 22:9-14)! God *always* keeps His promises. Even when nothing makes sense, choose confidence!

Lord, I choose to trust You to keep Your word.

Setback or Setup?

"God has made me forget all my trouble." . . .
"God has made me fruitful in the land of my suffering."
GENESIS 41:51-52 NIV

Joseph had multiple dreams that he'd rule over his parents and older brothers (Genesis 37:5-11). His brothers' jealousy caused them to sell Joseph as a slave. He worked faithfully for Potiphar, a captain of the guard in Egypt, but found himself in jail unfairly (Genesis 39). Although Joseph worked hard and honored God in his unjust circumstances, he still couldn't catch a break (Genesis 40). Joseph's life seemed to be one setback after another. But our setbacks are God's setups. God used every single unjust event to lead Joseph right where He wanted him—as Pharaoh's right-hand man (Genesis 45:5-8).

What setbacks have you faced? Have confidence that God knows exactly what He's doing—and that He's leading you right where He wants you.

Lord, help me be like Joseph. He faced so many setbacks,
but he never complained and never gave up. He still
honored You. Help me not to be discouraged but filled
with faith that You are guiding my every step.

Confident Belief

*It was by faith that Joseph, when he was about
to die, said confidently that the people of Israel
would leave Egypt. He even commanded them
to take his bones with them when they left.*

HEBREWS 11:22 NLT

God promised to give Abraham and his descendants a specific
portion of land that would be theirs forever (Genesis 13:14–17).
Joseph knew this, and he had total confidence that even though
all of Abraham's descendants were currently living in Egypt,
there would come a day when God would lead them all back
to the Promised Land. He was so confident that he made
his sons promise to take his bones with them when they left
(Genesis 50:24–26). And they did! Moses took Joseph's remains
with him when he led the Hebrews out of Egypt (Exodus 13:19).

What promise of God can you confidently claim, even
though your circumstances have not seen its fulfillment yet?
When God's promises are delayed, do you wallow in doubt
and despair or live in confident hope and expectation?

*God, help me live in confident belief like Joseph.
I want to totally trust Your promises.*

Confident Obedience

*The king of Egypt spoke to two Hebrew midwives named
Shiphrah and Puah: "When you are helping the Hebrew
women give birth and you see the baby being born, if it's
a boy, kill him. But if it's a girl, you can let her live." Now
the two midwives respected God so they didn't obey the
Egyptian king's order. Instead, they let the baby boys live.*

EXODUS 1:15–17 CEB

Shiphrah and Puah faced enormous pressure to obey a
command they knew was wrong. However, they respected
God's Law more than human law. They chose to put their
confidence in God. Their disobedience to the king caused
trouble, but God protected the women and rewarded them
for their faithfulness (Exodus 1:18–21).

Peer pressure or authoritative pressure can place us in
situations where following the rules means doing something
we know God says is wrong. We must choose: Will we give in
to pressure but disobey God—or obey God and risk human
consequences? Do you have the confidence to honor God
above anyone else?

*Lord, help me honor You above anyone else
and have the confidence to obey You, even if
that means facing human consequences.*

Facing the Giants

*"We saw there the Nephilim (the descendants of
Anak come from the Nephilim). We saw ourselves as
grasshoppers, and that's how we appeared to them."*

NUMBERS 13:33 CEB

The Lord commanded Moses to send spies into the Promised Land to scout before they battled for the land. The spies returned exclaiming about the fruit and abundance of the land (Numbers 13:23, 26–27). However, they also spread fear about the giants who lived there. "We can't attack those people! They're stronger than we are! They're all giants, and their cities are extremely fortified!" (see Numbers 13:28, 31–32). They *saw themselves* as grasshoppers next to their enemy, and they gave up before the battle even started.

Here's the deal: It doesn't matter how you see yourself—big, small, strong, or weak. It's how you see *God*. No matter how big and powerful the giants are in front of you, God is bigger and stronger. Choose to put your confidence in *Him*!

*God, I don't want my lack of confidence in myself
to make me quit before I even try. It's not about
me. It's really about my confidence in You.*

Paving the Way

"Do not be afraid or discouraged, for the LORD will personally go ahead of you. He will be with you; he will neither fail you nor abandon you."

DEUTERONOMY 31:8 NLT

The Israelites wandered in the desert for forty years as punishment for being afraid to enter the Promised Land. Now they stood at the edge of the Promised Land again. With one problem: the land was still occupied by enemy nations, and this rag-tag bunch of former slaves with no military experience had to march into the Promised Land and battle for it. No wonder God had to repeatedly tell them, "Be strong and courageous!" (Deuteronomy 31:7; Joshua 1:6, 7, 9).

Whenever you face circumstances that seem so much bigger than your ability, remember: the Lord personally goes ahead of you. He will pave the way for you, equip you, and work things out as only He can. Whether you're facing a major exam, an important game, or a group of bullies, find comfort knowing God goes before you.

Lord, please go before me today. I give my anxiety to You and choose to have courage and confidence instead. You are with me.

Step of Faith

During harvest the Jordan overflows its banks. When the priests carrying the Ark came to the edge of the river and stepped into the water, the water upstream stopped flowing. . . . So the people crossed the river near Jericho.

JOSHUA 3:15–16 NCV

When the Israelites fled Egypt, God miraculously parted the Red Sea (Exodus 14:21–22). Now they had to cross the Jordan River—which was flooded. God commanded them to cross (Joshua 1:2), but obedience wasn't so easy this time. With courage and complete trust in the Lord, the priests took the first step into the surging water. *Then* God miraculously parted the Jordan so the Israelites could cross.

Often we must take the first step of obedience in faith before we see God show up. What is God asking you to do? What first step of obedience do you need to take?

Lord, when You ask me to do tough things, help me remember Your faithfulness in the past so I can have courage to obey You now.

Remembrance Stones

*And Joshua set up at Gilgal the twelve stones they
had taken out of the Jordan. He said to the Israelites,
"In the future when your descendants ask their parents,
'What do these stones mean?' tell them, 'Israel crossed
the Jordan on dry ground.' For the LORD your God dried
up the Jordan before you until you had crossed over."*

JOSHUA 4:20–23 NIV

People in the Old Testament would often build altars or
monuments to remember a special moment with God (Genesis
12:7; 28:18–21). In the New Testament, Jesus also commanded
us to practice communion in remembrance of what He did on
the cross (1 Corinthians 11:24–25). These symbols served as
reminders so people would not forget the amazing work God
had done. They helped people keep their confidence in God.

When has God clearly revealed Himself to you or shown
His power in a mighty way? What symbol or tradition can you
create that will remind you of what God has done so your faith
in Him remains strong?

*Lord, help me remember what You've done in my
life as an encouragement to keep trusting You.*

Stay Strong!

"Your words have comforted those who fell, and you have strengthened those who could not stand. But now trouble comes to you, and you are discouraged; trouble hits you, and you are terrified. You should have confidence because you respect God; you should have hope because you are innocent."

JOB 4:4-6 NCV

Job's friend Eliphaz basically told Job: "Dude, take a dose of your own medicine." Job had comforted and encouraged many during their times of trouble. But now Job faced his own difficulty, and all his confidence in God went out the window. Has that ever happened to you? Sometimes it's easy to comfort and encourage others, but when trouble shows up on your doorstep, suddenly you don't find it so easy to trust God! The truths you share with others apply to you too. When pressure hits, don't let your confidence flee. Stay strong in what you know to be true, and stay steady in God's love and care.

God, help me not to lose my confidence when trouble hits. Strengthen me, and let the troubles I face deepen my trust in You.

Tired of Waiting

Saul waited there seven days for Samuel, as Samuel had instructed him earlier, but Samuel still didn't come. Saul realized that his troops were rapidly slipping away. So he demanded, "Bring me the burnt offering and the peace offerings!" And Saul sacrificed the burnt offering himself.

1 SAMUEL 13:8–9 NLT

Saul was a king (1 Samuel 13:1), not a priest. God clearly laid out rules for making sacrifices and who could perform them. But Saul grew impatient, so he made the sacrifice himself. Just as Saul was finishing the sacrifice, Samuel arrived. Saul immediately offered several excuses for jumping the gun. But Samuel wouldn't hear it. As a result of Saul's sin, he would be replaced as king (1 Samuel 13:10–14).

Have you ever grown impatient waiting on God's timing, so you *made* it happen? Getting ahead of God and handling things yourself can have very serious consequences. How are you tired of waiting on God? What do you desire that you should stop and ask God about first?

*God, help me wait on Your perfect timing
and give You the opportunity to move,
instead of controlling things myself.*

Proper Perspective

When the Israelites saw Goliath, every one of them ran away terrified of him. . . . David asked the soldiers standing by him, ". . .Who is that uncircumcised Philistine, anyway, that he can get away with insulting the army of the living God?"

1 SAMUEL 17:24, 26 CEB

The Israelites saw a nine-foot-nine giant who threatened them (1 Samuel 17:4). David saw a pagan peon who dared insult the living God and His chosen people. It's all in your perspective. You can focus on the giant and live in anxiety and terror. Or you can focus on Mighty God and put your confidence in Him. David, a teen, stood up to this giant when no one else would. Read his epic speech before he took Goliath down in 1 Samuel 17:45–47. Now that's some confidence!

What giant bully is blocking your path? How is the enemy trying to make you terrified? Put your confidence in Jesus, and stand your ground!

You are God Almighty! Nothing and no one can stand against You. When I'm tempted to run and hide in fear, adjust my perspective. Help me remember Your power and protection.

Unshakable

*The LORD is my light and my salvation—so why should
I be afraid? The LORD is my fortress, protecting me
from danger, so why should I tremble? . . . Though a
mighty army surrounds me, my heart will not be afraid.
Even if I am attacked, I will remain confident.*

PSALM 27:1, 3 NLT

Even if bad things happen. . .I will remain confident. How?!
Why?! David had no fear because of his total confidence
in God. He *knew* God in a deep, personal, intimate way—
like you know your best friend. Because David had such
deep confidence and trust in God, nothing he faced could
shake him.

How well do you know God? Is He more of an acquaintance
than a best friend? It's hard to trust a stranger you don't really
know. How can you start to know God better? If God is more
like a best friend, do you possess the same confidence David
had? What is causing you fear and anxiety right now? How can
what you know about God give you confidence and peace?

*Lord, help me know You better so I can
confidently face whatever happens.*

Teach Me, Lord

*Teach me how to live, O LORD. Lead me along the right
path, for my enemies are waiting for me. Do not let
me fall into their hands. For they accuse me of things
I've never done; with every breath they threaten me
with violence. Yet I am confident I will see the LORD's
goodness while I am here in the land of the living.*

PSALM 27:11–13 NLT

David faced a seriously unfair situation. People falsely accused
him in order to discredit him and take him down. Yet David's
reaction should give us pause. He didn't pick a fight or go
charging into the situation to defend himself. He turned to
God in prayer and sought the Lord's guidance. "Show me what
to do, Lord," he said. And he confidently believed God would.
Even though David was in the middle of lousy circumstances,
he firmly believed he would see God's goodness in the midst
of it. That confidence gave him peace and hope. When life
treats you unfairly, how do you respond? How can you be
more like David?

*Lord, help me control my tongue and turn to
You first when something unfair happens.*

Who Do You Trust?

*Then the Assyrian king's chief of staff told them to
give this message to Hezekiah: "This is what
the great king of Assyria says: What are you
trusting in that makes you so confident?"*

2 KINGS 18:19 NLT

The king of Assyria and his mighty army surrounded Jerusalem.
King Hezekiah and the Israelites were trapped. Assyria was
the most powerful nation at the time, and no nation could
stand against them. The Israelites were doomed—but they
put their confidence in God. Immediately King Hezekiah
went to the temple and prayed to the Lord (2 Kings 19:14-19).
God answered and drove the Assyrian army away Himself
(2 Kings 19:35-37).

What are you trusting in that makes you so confident?
The king of Assyria trusted in himself—in his own power and
military might. He didn't need God because he thought his
abilities were enough. True confidence comes in trusting God
alone—even in the most impossible circumstances. Where
do you put your confidence?

*Lord, forgive me for trusting in myself.
Help me always put my trust in You because
I can confidently depend on You—every time.*

Do Not Comply

But Daniel was determined not to defile himself by eating the food and wine given to them by the king. He asked the chief of staff for permission not to eat these unacceptable foods.

DANIEL 1:8 NLT

Babylon had defeated the Israelites and carried Daniel off as a prisoner. Daniel had been brought to the king's palace in Babylon, where he was to be stripped of his culture and indoctrinated in Babylonian beliefs and customs. But Daniel knew the foods given to him were against God's Law. He refused to let his faith values be stripped away. Risking his life, he confidently and respectfully did not conform. Daniel took the first step of faith, *then* God honored him by showing favor and making a way (Daniel 1:9–20).

Today's culture increasingly wants to strip you of your faith values. Christian beliefs are not popular. Are you determined, like Daniel, to follow God—no matter what? Will you confidently not conform to the world and trust God with the results?

Lord, give me courage to stand up for my faith and not give in to the pressures to conform. Help me trust You with the results.

Confident Rescue

*The three men replied, "Your Majesty, we don't
need to defend ourselves. The God we worship
can save us from you and your flaming furnace.
But even if he doesn't, we still won't worship your
gods and the gold statue you have set up."*

DANIEL 3:16–18 CEV

The Babylonian king made an image of gold ninety feet high
and nine feet wide and commanded everyone to worship the
statue—or be thrown into a blazing furnace (Daniel 3:1–6).
But Shadrach, Meshach, and Abednego refused to obey the
king's command and were reported to the king (Daniel 3:8–12).
Furious, King Nebuchadnezzar gave them one last opportunity
to bow in worship, but they boldly refused. They knew God
could save them, *but even if He didn't*, they still refused to
worship another god. That's confidence! Their trust in God
was so complete, they were willing to die to do the right thing.
God can rescue you. But if He doesn't, do you still possess
the confidence to follow Him?

*Lord, You are so worthy of my devotion and trust. You
sacrificed Your life for me. I give my life to You in return.*

Confident Courage

Esther sent Mordecai this reply: "Go and get all the Jews in Susa together; hold a fast and pray for me. Don't eat or drink anything for three days and nights. My servant women and I will be doing the same. After that, I will go to the king, even though it is against the law. If I must die for doing it, I will die."

ESTHER 4:15-16 GNT

An evil plot had been hatched to massacre all the Jews (Esther 3:8-11). Mordecai went straight to Queen Esther, a Jew, telling her to help her people and plead for the king's mercy. But Esther knew approaching the king without being summoned meant death (Esther 4:10-11). She gathered her courage, spent three days in prayer and fasting, then put her confidence in God and approached the king.

God places us in specific positions for a purpose. And sometimes that purpose requires an enormous amount of courage. If God is asking you to take a step of faith, will you follow Esther's example and spend time in focused prayer then confidently obey?

*Lord, give me courage and confidence
to obey You even when it's hard.*

Confident Restoration

*Just then a woman who had been subject to bleeding
for twelve years came up behind him and touched the
edge of his cloak. She said to herself, "If I only touch
his cloak, I will be healed." Jesus turned and saw her.
"Take heart, daughter," he said, "your faith has healed
you." And the woman was healed at that moment.*

MATTHEW 9:20–22 NIV

This woman had been ritually unclean for *twelve* years.
According to Jewish law, she had been living in complete
isolation from society. The Bible tells us this woman "had
suffered a great deal under the care of many doctors and
had spent all she had, yet instead of getting better she grew
worse" (Mark 5:26 NIV). Imagine her complete desperation
and despair as she snuck up behind Jesus. She literally had
no other hope. But Jesus wouldn't let her sneak away. He
turned and *saw* her—her weary heart as well as her broken
body. He claimed her as His own, calling her daughter, and
healed her. Jesus sees you and your circumstances as well.
Run to Him to find hope and restoration.

*Jesus, You are my hope. I desperately
need You. Please restore. . . .*

Persistent Faith

*A Canaanite woman from that vicinity came to
him, crying out, "Lord, Son of David, have mercy
on me! My daughter is demon-possessed and
suffering terribly." Jesus did not answer a word.*

MATTHEW 15:22–23 NIV

Canaanites, especially, were considered enemies of Israel. So
this enemy foreign woman approached Jesus and asked for
a miracle. And He ignored her. But she kept asking. Finally
Jesus answered her and said, "I'm only here for the Jews."
Undeterred, she knelt before Him and cried out, "Lord, help
me!" (see Matthew 15:23–25).

The knowledge she had of Jesus gave her enough
confidence in Him to persistently seek His help. Racial barriers
didn't stop her. Her limited knowledge didn't stop her. Jesus'
initial silence didn't stop her. Jesus praised her great faith and
healed her daughter (Matthew 15:28). Jesus initially remained
silent, not because He didn't care. He delayed His response to
allow her trusting faith to grow. Would she give up? Or would
she confidently pursue Him? The woman chose confidence.

*Lord, even when You're silent, even when I face so
many obstacles, I choose to put my trust in You.*

Honest Questions

When John, who was in prison, heard about the deeds of the Messiah, he sent his disciples to ask him, "Are you the one who is to come, or should we expect someone else?"

MATTHEW 11:2–3 NIV

John the Baptist, Jesus' own cousin, experienced a crisis of faith. John surely knew the prophecies surrounding his birth and Jesus' birth (Luke 1). John knew he was the forerunner to the Messiah—his job was to call Israel to repentance and make them ready to receive the Messiah. John believed Jesus was this Messiah (Matthew 3:13–15). But as time passed, Jesus didn't meet the expectations John had of who the Messiah would be and what He would do. Suddenly, he doubted. So he went straight to Jesus and asked his hard questions.

It's completely normal for circumstances to create doubt. Everyone wrestles with it. Go straight to God with your uncertainties. You can be confident God is strong enough to handle your hard questions.

Lord, sometimes it's hard to believe You and trust You. Grow my faith in You as I wrestle with my questions. Show me what's true.

Sinking Faith

Then Peter called to him, "Lord, if it's really you, tell me to come to you, walking on the water." "Yes, come," Jesus said. So Peter went over the side of the boat and walked on the water toward Jesus. But when he saw the strong wind and the waves, he was terrified and began to sink. "Save me, Lord!" he shouted. Jesus immediately reached out and grabbed him. "You have so little faith," Jesus said. "Why did you doubt me?"

MATTHEW 14:28–31 NLT

Peter had some major confidence in Jesus. If Jesus walked on water, he could too! But as soon as Peter took his eyes off Jesus and focused on the terrifying problem, he let fear replace his confidence. So he sank.

When we let our fear become bigger than our God, our faith sinks. No matter what circumstances surround us, God is bigger! "But it's impossible!" you say. With God, all things are possible (Matthew 19:26). Is Jesus truly bigger to you than anything you face? Then choose to put your trust in Him, and walk on that water, girl!

No more fear. God, today I choose to trust You.

Do What You Can

*"She did what she could. She poured perfume on my
body beforehand to prepare for my burial. Truly I tell you,
wherever the gospel is preached throughout the world,
what she has done will also be told, in memory of her."*

MARK 14:8–9 NIV

The disciples rebuked Mary harshly for "wasting" an expensive
jar of perfume (Mark 14:3–5). But Mary understood what
the disciples still couldn't grasp. Jesus was about to die,
and she wanted to anoint Him for His burial. In a gesture of
love, she took what she had and did what she could.

That's all Jesus asks of you. You don't have to save the
world or evangelize everyone you see. You don't have to
exhaust yourself doing things for Jesus or carry a niggling
sense of guilt that you're never doing *enough*. Take the gifts
and resources God has given you and do what you can. That's
sufficient.

*Jesus, I love You and want to serve You, but so many
times I don't feel like it's enough. Help me do what I can
and let go of the guilt and weight of not doing more.*

In or Out?

Then he cursed and swore, "I don't know the man!" At that very moment the rooster crowed. Peter remembered Jesus' words, "Before the rooster crows you will deny me three times." And Peter went out and cried uncontrollably.

MATTHEW 26:74-75 CEB

Peter was an all-in kind of guy. He even had the courage to climb out of a boat during a storm and walk on water—because he believed Jesus could do anything. But suddenly following Jesus got really hard. The disciples expected Jesus to be a political Messiah, overthrow Rome, and set up His own righteous kingdom. Yet Jesus was being arrested, beaten, and sentenced to death. Peter couldn't understand what was happening. And in his confusion, he basically said, "I'm out!"

Life doesn't always go as planned. When things take a sharp turn, it's easy to get confused, be filled with doubt, and maybe even desire to walk away from God. But you can have confidence in God's sovereignty. He's in control. He knows what He's doing. You can trust Him.

Jesus, help me trust You, even when nothing makes sense.

God's Love for Women

Mary Magdalene went and said to the followers, "I saw the Lord!" And she told them what Jesus had said to her.
JOHN 20:18 NCV

God chose Mary Magdalene to be the first person to see Jesus resurrected and to tell the others He had risen from the dead. Both Peter and John had explored the empty tomb (John 20:3-9). But Jesus waited until they left to appear to Mary (John 20:10-11). In that culture, a woman's testimony meant nothing. It held no weight or value. Yet God entrusted the greatest news of all time not to His prized disciples—but to a woman.

Women are not overlooked by Jesus, and neither are you. You are special and precious to Him. He sees you and wants to reveal Himself to you. When the pressure hit, Peter denied Jesus three times, but Mary never abandoned Jesus; she stayed with Him to the cross (Luke 22:56-62; John 19:25). Follow her example of faithfulness and be confident of your value and worth to God!

Jesus, thank You for valuing me just as much as men. Help me remain faithful to You.

Stay Focused

When Peter saw [John], he asked, "Lord, what about him?" Jesus answered, "If I want him to remain alive until I return, what is that to you? You must follow me."

JOHN 21:21-22 NIV

After Jesus' resurrection, He reinstated Peter as the leader of the disciples and gave him his mission, even hinting at Peter's death (John 21:15-19). What did Peter do? Turned and asked, "What about him? Is he going to die too?" Jesus gently rebuked him and said, "Don't worry about other people. Keep your eyes focused on Me and do what I told you to do."

God will ask us to do hard things at times—to give something up, say no to an opportunity, or do something we don't want to do. Like Peter, we often immediately compare. "Why doesn't she have to give this up? Why does he get to go?" But the proper response is to stay focused on Jesus and obey what He's called you to do.

Lord, help me not to compare and feel resentful but to stay focused on what You want me to do. Help me be willing to obey right away.

Peter's Peace

*The night before Herod was to bring him to trial, Peter
was sleeping between two soldiers. . . . Suddenly an
angel of the Lord appeared and a light shone in the cell.
He struck Peter on the side and woke him up. "Quick,
get up!" he said, and the chains fell off Peter's wrists.*

ACTS 12:6-7 NIV

King Herod was none too happy with Christians. He had just
killed the apostle James (Acts 12:2), and Peter was next. Peter
waited in jail the night before his execution, and what was he
doing? *Sleeping!* So deeply, in fact, the angel whacked him
to wake him up.

What would you do the night before your impending
death? Have a panic attack, drowning in fear and anxiety?
Not Peter. He had so much confidence and trust in Jesus, he
didn't worry a bit. He knew his life was in God's hands, so
he slept in peace. When you're tempted to freak out, take a
lesson from Peter. God's got this!

*Wow, God, the confidence Peter had in You
amazes me. Help me have that same confidence
and place my trust in You with total peace.*

Mentally Tough

We and the people there pleaded with Paul not to go up to Jerusalem. Then Paul answered, "Why are you weeping and breaking my heart? I am ready not only to be bound, but also to die in Jerusalem for the name of the Lord Jesus."

ACTS 21:12-13 NIV

Paul decided to travel to Jerusalem in obedience to the Spirit. But this was no happy vacation. The Spirit warned Paul that prison and hardships waited for him there (Acts 20:22–24). Can you imagine the resolve and courage Paul possessed to obey that command from the Lord? Even Paul's friends wept and pleaded with him not to go. But Paul refused to ride the highs and lows of emotions. He remained mentally steady—fixing his eyes on Jesus (Hebrews 12:2–3).

When you are called to hard things, how do you respond? Do you let your emotions influence your obedience? Do you let friends talk you out of it? Or do you place all your confidence and trust in Jesus, no matter what happens?

God, help me place all my confidence and trust in You alone. Help me fix my eyes on You.

Costly Obedience

The following night the Lord stood near Paul and said, "Take courage! As you have testified about me in Jerusalem, so you must also testify in Rome."

ACTS 23:11 NIV

Sure enough, Paul made it to Jerusalem, but about a week later a mob severely beat him and Roman soldiers arrested him (Acts 21:17–22:29). Attacked, bruised, and bloody, Paul lay in his jail cell. In that moment, the Lord appeared to Paul, *stood near*, and comforted him. Paul's obedience cost a lot. But Jesus didn't abandon Paul to face it alone.

Following Christ is not easy. Sometimes He asks a lot. But He never abandons us. When times get tough, He's right there beside you, walking through it with you. He'll never ask you to do something and then let you face the fire alone. How has God shown Himself to you in the past? How can that give you courage to obey Him today?

Jesus, thank You for never abandoning me.
Following You can be really difficult sometimes.
Help me feel Your presence with me as I obey You.

Detour Ahead!

"Be still, and know that I am God."

PSALM 46:10 NIV

Paul had planned many times to visit Rome, but plans changed and he never made it (Romans 1:13). Now, finally, he was on his way to Rome—in chains, as a prisoner. Paul could easily have said, "Uh, God, this is not how I saw this going!" But he allowed God to be Lord of all the unexpected turns. Even his trip to Rome detoured many times (Acts 27:1-12). His boat shipwrecked and everyone nearly died (Acts 27:13-44), then they unexpectedly wintered on an island (Acts 28:1-11). Paul remained calm and flexible, trusting God to control the direction of his life.

When unexpected twists hit your life, how do you respond? Do fear and anxiety overwhelm you? Do you rant and let God know how upset you are? Or can you remain calm, knowing God is in full control and He's got this?

Lord, when life takes a sudden turn and blindsides me, help me not to freak out. Help me remember that You're in control of every detour and nothing surprises You. Help me rest in Your sovereignty.

Finish Line

As for me, my life has already been poured out as an offering to God. The time of my death is near. I have fought the good fight, I have finished the race, and I have remained faithful. And now the prize awaits me—the crown of righteousness, which the Lord, the righteous Judge, will give me on the day of his return.

2 TIMOTHY 4:6-8 NLT

Paul arrived in Rome, witnessed there, and knew he would die there. Even facing death, Paul remained confident. He could see the finish line, and he knew he'd run a good race. Jesus would be waiting for Paul with a crown, and Paul could live his last days with hope and comfort—even though he remained in jail.

No one is guaranteed a long life. We are not even promised we will live another day. How confident are you about facing death? Do you feel you've run a good race so far and remained faithful? If not, what course corrections do you need to make?

Lord, I want my life to mean something. Show me how You want me to serve You and run the race You've marked for me.

Confidence Builder

And I want you to know, my dear brothers and sisters,
that everything that has happened to me here has helped
to spread the Good News. For everyone here, including
the whole palace guard, knows that I am in chains
because of Christ. And because of my imprisonment,
most of the believers here have gained confidence
and boldly speak God's message without fear.

PHILIPPIANS 1:12-14 NLT

Paul's example gave other believers confidence. He fearlessly shared the Gospel with everyone around him. His complete trust in God made Paul confident that his circumstances were orchestrated by God to put him where he needed to be to spread the Gospel to people who needed it. His boldness and confidence in the midst of suffering gave other believers the same courage. They too began to boldly share the Gospel without fear.

Your courage and example can be the confidence builder other Christians need. If you're in need of some confidence yourself, who can you draw courage from—either in the Bible or in your life?

Lord, Paul was so courageous. His strong confidence
in You was infectious and gave others boldness.
Give me that same confidence and courage.

I Don't Get It!

*Trust in and rely confidently on the LORD with all
your heart and do not rely on your own insight or
understanding. In all your ways know and acknowledge
and recognize Him, and He will make your paths straight
and smooth [removing obstacles that block your way].*

PROVERBS 3:5-6 AMP

Sometimes God asks us to do things that make *no* sense. Commanding a bunch of abused ex-slaves to battle against giants in heavily fortified cities? Say what?! Maybe like the Israelites, you feel pure terror about what God is leading you to do. Or maybe like Abraham with Isaac, God will ask you to sacrifice something that doesn't seem to go along with His promises.

You can reason yourself out of obedience Every. Single. Time. But if everything made sense, it wouldn't take trust. We wouldn't need to rely on God because we could rely confidently on our own understanding. How are you struggling to trust God because things don't make sense to you?

*Lord, I give up control. I lay down my desire to
understand, and I submit to You. I will trust You and
rely confidently on You rather than my own insight.*

Worldly Concerns

Don't love the world or anything that belongs to the world.
If you love the world, you cannot love the Father. Our foolish
pride comes from this world, and so do our selfish desires
and our desire to have everything we see. None of this
comes from the Father. The world and the desires it causes
are disappearing. But if we obey God, we will live forever.

1 JOHN 2:15–17 CEV

Every day you face a choice: put your confidence in the world
or put your confidence in Christ. Which matters more to you?
That you keep up with the trendy fashions and own all the
same fancy gadgets as your friends? Or that you're a girl of
character who cares more about what God thinks of you?
How much time do you spend on apps and social media?
How many selfies do you take and post? Take an honest look
at your life. How much of what the world offers do you desire
and pursue? What does obedience to God look like for you?

Father, please forgive me for my pride and selfish desires.
Show me how You want me to obey You today.

It's Not Fair!

The payment for sin is death. But God gives us the
free gift of life forever in Christ Jesus our Lord.
ROMANS 6:23 NCV

Life is not fair. It's just not. We can whine about it, cry about it, rebel against it. . .or accept it. Let me tell you a secret: you don't want life to be fair. Wanna know why? Because in all fairness, you deserve death. We all do. Our sin should land us squarely in hell. That's what's fair. But God in His mercy took our place; Jesus paid that penalty for us. Because of His free grace, we can be restored with God and enjoy eternal life with Him forever. Was Jesus' death on the cross fair? No. But He chose to accept that path anyway.

Are you holding a grudge because something isn't fair? Let it go. Grace has been shown to you. Extend that grace to others around you.

Jesus, You endured the cross for me, and that's totally
not fair. I deserved that punishment. Help me show
others the same love and grace You show me.

Growing Pains

*My brothers and sisters, when you have many kinds
of troubles, you should be full of joy, because you
know that these troubles test your faith, and this
will give you patience. Let your patience show itself
perfectly in what you do. Then you will be perfect
and complete and will have everything you need.*

JAMES 1:2–4 NCV

No one likes problems. They cause stress, anxiety, depression, tension, and frustration. And James said we're supposed to be full of joy about that? What planet was he from?

Joy is different than happiness. Happiness comes and goes with your emotions. Joy is the deep, abiding state of gratefulness and contentment unaffected by circumstances. You can have joy while tears of grief stream down your face. So although troubles are never fun, we can be joyful because we know God is allowing them to grow and mature us. You can be confident each problem in your life has a purpose. How is God growing you today?

*Lord, thank You for the problems in my life.
Help me respond well and trust You. I know
You're using them to grow my faith and mature me.*

Jesus Never Fails

It is better to trust the LORD for protection than
to trust anyone else, including strong leaders.

PSALM 118:8-9 CEV

People fail us. We can tell story after story of how we trusted someone and they didn't come through. The only Person who will never fail you is Jesus. Do you place your confidence in other people? Are you looking to a certain person to rescue you, protect you, provide for you, fix your problems, or make you happy? People may fulfill us for a while, but it never lasts. You can hop from person to person, but no one will fully meet your needs.

Only Jesus is worthy of our complete confidence. Who do you depend on to protect you? How do you try to find satisfaction in other people? Take those needs to Jesus and trust Him to fulfill those desires for you.

Lord, it's easy to look to friends or leaders or family
members to meet my needs. It's also easy to feel
depressed or angry when they don't. Today I put
my confidence totally in You. I ask that You protect
me, that You fulfill my needs and desires.

No Fear

So we can say with confidence, "The LORD is my helper,
so I will have no fear. What can mere people do to me?"

HEBREWS 13:6 NLT

Uh, people can do a lot! They can brutalize you on social
media and online. They can bully you and make your life a
living hell. People can force you to do things you don't want
to do. They can even take your life. And we're not supposed
to fear any of that?! Nope, we're not. Because when you have
so much confidence in God, the fear disappears. Sure, people
can do a lot of bodily and emotional harm, but they can't
touch your soul (Matthew 10:28). Even death is a win for us
because we'll be present with Christ (Philippians 1:20–21).

Are you fully confident in the Lord as your Helper? Do
you trust Him to care for and protect you? To walk with you
in the valley of the shadow of death (Psalm 23:4)? What
fears do you need to surrender to Him?

Lord, I give my fears to You. I choose to trust
You and put my confidence in You, my Helper.

Thorny Distractions

"The seed that fell among the thorns represents those who hear God's word, but all too quickly the message is crowded out by the worries of this life and the lure of wealth, so no fruit is produced."

MATTHEW 13:22 NLT

Are your times with God fruitful? Do you read these devotions, feel God speaking to you, then have changed behavior as a result? Or do you simply read a devotion, slap the book closed ("Did my devotion today! Check!"), and go about your normal life?

Jesus wants our hearts to be good soil, where we receive and understand God's Word and it changes us (Matthew 13:23). But it's super easy to let the worries of life crowd out our time with God: "I'm so busy! Homework, practice, friends, and. . . and my social media!" Things in life will *always* demand your attention. But don't let them distract you or lure you away from spending intentional, meaningful, fruitful time with God.

Lord, show me what's distracting me from You. Help me not to see these devotions as a chore to be checked off, but as meaningful time to grow my relationship with You.

Strike! It's Out!

*His peace will guard your hearts and
minds as you live in Christ Jesus.*
PHILIPPIANS 4:7 NLT

Let peace be your umpire. Does scrolling your social media pages cause discontent, jealousy, and bitterness? That's not peace. Strike! It's out! Are you doing an activity because it brings you joy or it aids in your growth? Or are you simply doing it because you feel you should and so it feels more like a burden? Peace says it's out! Do you hate the chores your parents give you? Sorry, peace says those are safe—because obeying your parents means peace in your relationship.

As you focus more and more of your attention on Jesus, He will guide you with His peace. Take a break from—or maybe completely give up—the things in your life that are causing unhealthy emotions or behavior. You might find your life is a whole lot more peaceful without them!

*Lord, thank You for guarding my heart and mind
with Your peace. Show me what's unhealthy in
my life and what You want me to change.*

Final Roll Call

"The Son of Man will send out his angels, and they will gather from his kingdom everyone who does wrong or causes others to sin. Then he will throw them into a flaming furnace, where people will cry and grit their teeth in pain. But everyone who has done right will shine like the sun in their Father's kingdom. If you have ears, pay attention!"

MATTHEW 13:41-43 CEV

You can be confident there will be a final judgment (Revelation 20:11-15). Those who trust in Christ for salvation will receive mercy because the punishment due us for our sin was already paid by Him. The only judgment Christians face will be an evaluation of their service to Jesus during their lives (2 Corinthians 5:10; 1 Corinthians 3:14). However, those who reject Jesus will face eternal punishment (2 Thessalonians 1:7-10).

Your actions matter. You cannot escape accountability. This helps us gain perspective on what's truly important and properly motivates us to share the Gospel.

Lord, help me be more concerned about serving You and sharing You with others than the silly things in this life that don't matter.

Total Surrender

When Jesus heard this, he said to him, "You still
lack one thing. Sell everything you have and give
to the poor, and you will have treasure in heaven.
Then come, follow me." When he heard this, he
became very sad, because he was very wealthy.

LUKE 18:22–23 NIV

A ruler approached Jesus and asked Him how to inherit eternal life. The ruler had kept all the commandments of the Law since he was a young boy, but Jesus said he still lacked one thing: he loved his wealth more than God. Is it a sin to be wealthy? No! But it's a sin to love *anything* or *anyone* more than God. And the ruler wasn't willing to give up his wealth and follow Jesus.

Is there something or someone you love more than God? Something you haven't been willing to give up or surrender? Jesus wants it all. You can be confident that surrendering everything to Jesus will bring unimaginable rewards—in this life and eternity.

Lord, I surrender _____ to You. You are more
important to me than anything else. I will follow You.

Holy Hug

God is our merciful Father and the source of all comfort. He comforts us in all our troubles so that we can comfort others. When they are troubled, we will be able to give them the same comfort God has given us. . . . We are confident that as you share in our sufferings, you will also share in the comfort God gives us.

2 CORINTHIANS 1:3–4, 7 NLT

God allows bad things to happen for two reasons: (1) so you will seek Him, and (2) so He can equip you to share His comfort with others as a testimony to Him. When you face hard events, it often drives you to Jesus. Your tough circumstances become a training ground for your faith. The Lord has things to teach you about Himself—things you can only learn during a tough spiritual workout. Life might suck, but you can be confident God is there to comfort you.

What's really tough right now? Have you turned to Jesus for help and comfort? How has He comforted you?

Merciful Father, I need Your comfort. Please wrap Your arms around me and hold me tight.

In Over Your Head

We think you ought to know, dear brothers and sisters, about the trouble we went through in the province of Asia. We were crushed and overwhelmed beyond our ability to endure, and we thought we would never live through it. In fact, we expected to die. But as a result, we stopped relying on ourselves and learned to rely only on God, who raises the dead. And he did rescue us from mortal danger, and he will rescue us again. We have placed our confidence in him, and he will continue to rescue us.

2 CORINTHIANS 1:8–10 NLT

"God will not give you more than you can bear." Have you heard that common phrase among Christians? It's a lie! It's true that God will not allow you to be *tempted* beyond your ability to resist (1 Corinthians 10:13), but He absolutely will allow you to face circumstances that are so beyond your ability to handle. Why? So you can learn to stop relying on yourself and rely on Him. It's not about YOU. It's about HIM.

Lord, I surrender my confidence in myself,
and I put my confidence in You alone.

Share with Confidence

This is the confidence that we have through Christ in the presence of God. It isn't that we ourselves are qualified to claim that anything came from us. No, our qualification is from God.

2 CORINTHIANS 3:4–5 CEB

Jesus commanded His followers to share the Gospel with everyone (Matthew 28:19). As His representatives, we are His agents to share the Good News to those who are lost and dying. "But I'm not qualified!" you say. "I'm still learning. I don't know what to say!" The truth is you *are* qualified because the Holy Spirit lives inside you. That's the only qualification needed. He will give you the words to say (Mark 13:11). He does all the work in other people's hearts. He just needs you to be His witness. Share the Gospel with confidence. It's not about how adequate you are; it's about how adequate Jesus is!

Lord, sometimes I feel so inadequate sharing the Gospel. Plus, it's kinda scary because I don't want to feel rejected or teased. But the Gospel isn't about me. It's about You and Your powerful work on the cross. So help me share with confidence and boldness.

Above and Beyond

*I am confident as I write this letter that
you will do what I ask and even more!*

PHILEMON V. 21 NLT

Do people have that same confidence in you? Are you responsible, reliable, and a person who goes above and beyond? Could your parents say this about you? Being a person of character is important. Completing tasks—and completing them well—not only reflects well on you but also reflects well on Jesus. "Work willingly at whatever you do, as though you were working for the Lord rather than for people" (Colossians 3:23 NLT). Ultimately, Jesus is our Master, and our work ethic should be worthy of Him. How have you been slacking lately? Where do you need to have a better attitude about what's being asked of you? How does seeing Jesus as your Master (instead of your parents, teachers, or coaches) help change your perspective?

*Lord, help me put the same diligence into my efforts
for others as I would for You. Help me have a good
attitude and go above and beyond what's expected
because I know it will bless others and please You.*

Zip It!

Do everything without complaining and arguing,
so that no one can criticize you. Live clean, innocent
lives as children of God, shining like bright lights
in a world full of crooked and perverse people.
PHILIPPIANS 2:14–15 NLT

Ouch. This is a hard one. Do *some* things without complaining and arguing? Do *only the things I want to do* without complaining and arguing? No, do *everything* without complaining and arguing. That means no complaints about doing your homework, chores, and extra duties your parents give you. It means no arguing when your parents tell you to turn off the TV or take a break from your phone.

God wants us to have cheerful hearts. When you're tempted to complain or argue, try responding with an attitude of gratitude. I know, I know. . .that's so *opposite* of how you feel, but give it a try! Responding with a smile, a cheerful "sure!" or maybe even a thank-you to your parents or others for all the hard work they do will truly make you stand out as a bright light.

Looooord, I need help with this one! Help me not to
complain or argue but to be loving and grateful.

Safe Boundaries

"If you obey my decrees and my regulations,
you will find life through them. I am the LORD."

LEVITICUS 18:5 NLT

Rules, rules, rules! Sometimes you get *so tired* of all the rules! You imagine life will be so much better once you're on your own and don't have to live under your parents' rules anymore. Satan likes to make us resent God's rules too. He likes to distort God as a total killjoy who's super strict and who loves to make your life miserable by imposing rules that take away all your freedom and fun. But that's so far from the truth!

Parents use baby gates to let their young children roam free in a safe area. The gates protect from danger and harm, and parents use them because they love their children and are attentive to their care. God's rules are the same: born from a heart of love for you, to protect you from danger and harm, to give you life and freedom inside the boundaries of what's good and safe.

Lord, I know Your rules have a purpose. Help me
value and obey them instead of resent them.

Clear Conscience

*We can say with confidence and a clear conscience
that we have lived with a God-given holiness and
sincerity in all our dealings. We have depended on
God's grace, not on our own human wisdom. That is
how we have conducted ourselves before the world.*

2 CORINTHIANS 1:12 NLT

Can you say the same thing with confidence? Have you lived a holy lifestyle—one of integrity, honesty, and sincerity? Have your motives been pure? How's your conduct been with your parents? Siblings? Friends? Teachers? Do kids at school see something different in you because you don't act like them? If you feel the Holy Spirit pricking your conscience, take a minute to listen to Him. Is He asking you to do something or say something to someone? Is there something you need to apologize for or make right? Don't give in to the temptation to justify your actions or rationalize your behavior. If the Holy Spirit is nudging you, it's wise to listen and repent.

*God, help me live today with integrity and sincerity
so at the end of the day I can say with confidence
and a clear conscience that I have lived God's way.*

Confidence in Community

Some people have given up the habit of meeting for
worship, but we must not do that. We should keep on
encouraging each other, especially since you know
that the day of the Lord's coming is getting closer.

HEBREWS 10:25 CEV

The good news is you're not meant to follow Jesus alone. We need community for support and accountability. The Bible tells us we need to meet regularly for worship and to encourage each other. We should be part of a church family that is devoted to studying God's Word and praying for each other, not just a church social club that plays games and serves snacks (Acts 2:42). Church should be a place where we experience the unity of the Spirit—where we lay aside the divisions of the world and unite in peace (Ephesians 4:2–6)

Are you regularly attending a solid church or youth group? If not, explore some options with your parents or visit a friend's church. It's a lot easier to walk confidently when you have a band of friends walking with you!

Lord, as busy as my schedule can be,
help me value and prioritize going to church.

Confidence in the Cross

We put no confidence in human effort, though I could have confidence in my own effort if anyone could. Indeed, if others have reason for confidence in their own efforts, I have even more!

PHILIPPIANS 3:3-4 NLT

Salvation and God's favor are not earned. Paul knew this. He did everything right, strictly obeyed the Law, and came from a pure Jewish bloodline (Philippians 3:5-6). But "I no longer count on my own righteousness through obeying the law; rather, I become righteous through faith in Christ," Paul said (Philippians 3:9 NLT).

Faithful church attendance, youth group involvement, or daily Bible reading does not save you. Completing religious rites of passage like confirmation and baptism doesn't save you. While these are all good things, we can't put our confidence in them to earn God's favor. It's not about what we do; it's about what Jesus did on the cross. Our confidence is in Him. How are you tempted to earn God's favor and put confidence in your own righteousness?

Lord, forgive me for counting on my own effort, thinking I deserve Your favor because I'm so good. I'm already enough because You are enough.

Confidence in Grace

Then Jesus said, "Come to me, all of you who are weary and carry heavy burdens, and I will give you rest. Take my yoke upon you. Let me teach you, because I am humble and gentle at heart, and you will find rest for your souls. For my yoke is easy to bear, and the burden I give you is light."

MATTHEW 11:28–30 NLT

The Jewish people had become burdened with the heaviness of the Law. Jewish Law combined rules from the Old Testament with additional rules the religious leaders heaped on top. Obeying all those commands was hard work! Then Jesus arrived and lived a perfect life—obeying *every single rule*. He kept the Law and sacrificed Himself on the cross so we could be free from the heavy burden of a works-based religion. He offers us grace—free and clear. You don't have to work for it. You don't have to earn it. How are you still working for God's favor? Choose to be confident in God's grace.

Thank You, Jesus, for taking the heavy burden of the Law and giving me the light yoke of grace.

Confidence in Eternal Life

I have been sent to proclaim faith to those God has chosen and to teach them to know the truth that shows them how to live godly lives. This truth gives them confidence that they have eternal life, which God—who does not lie—promised them before the world began.

TITUS 1:1-2 NLT

The entire basis of our Christian faith is the reality of eternal life with God. Adam and Eve broke that eternal relationship when they sinned. Jesus took our sin's punishment when He died on the cross in order to restore our eternal relationship with God. Too often we get bogged down in the daily details and drama of our lives, not really thinking about heaven. But our time on earth is just a temporary phase. Our true citizenship is in heaven (Philippians 3:20).

Are you confident you have eternal life with God? If not, who can answer your questions? What hope does the promise of eternal life give you? How can that hope change your perspective as you go through this day?

Lord, set my mind on heavenly things and not on earthly matters.

Confidence in God's Promises

So God has given both his promise and his oath. These two things are unchangeable because it is impossible for God to lie. Therefore, we who have fled to him for refuge can have great confidence as we hold to the hope that lies before us. This hope is a strong and trustworthy anchor for our souls.

HEBREWS 6:18-19 NLT

The author of Hebrews encouraged his readers not to have a lazy faith but to "be like those who believe and are patient, and so receive what God has promised" (Hebrews 6:12 GNT). God promised Abraham many descendants, and Abraham waited twenty-five years for God to fulfill this promise.

We too can cling to God's promises as an anchor for our souls. When you're tempted to doubt God's faithfulness, when you're impatient with waiting and want to take matters into your own hands and do things your way, let the strong and trustworthy promises of God give you confidence. What promise do you need to cling to today?

Lord, help me believe and be patient while I believe. May Your promises hold me steady.

Confidence in Jesus' Return

*They said, "Men of Galilee, why are you standing
here looking into the sky? Jesus, whom you
saw taken up from you into heaven, will come
back in the same way you saw him go."*

ACTS 1:11 NCV

Jesus is coming back, y'all! Almost two thousand years have passed since Jesus returned to heaven, but you can be confident He *is* coming back someday. He left the Holy Spirit as an engagement ring—a promise and guarantee of what's to come (2 Corinthians 5:5). When the full number of believers have put their trust in Him (Romans 11:25), Jesus will return for His bride, the Church (1 Thessalonians 4:16-17). He will take us into heaven for the wedding supper of the Lamb, where we will celebrate our eternal spiritual uniting with God (Revelation 19:6-9).

Jesus told us to keep watch and be ready for His return (Matthew 24:42-51). Are you ready? If Jesus returns tomorrow, how would that change how you live today?

*Jesus, I'm so excited for You to come back!
Help me set the right priorities while I wait for You.*

Confidence in Compassion

*When they came to Jesus, they saw the man who
had been possessed by the legion of demons,
sitting there, dressed and in his right mind.*

MARK 5:15 NIV

Jesus healed a man who the world thought was a hopeless case. This isn't the first or only time Jesus' compassion led Him to fulfill the Isaiah 61 prophecy to proclaim good news to the poor, freedom for the prisoners, and recovery of sight for the blind and to set the oppressed free (Luke 4:18-19). Jesus was confident in this mission of compassion that brought people who didn't know God to a saving faith (Romans 2:4). He never wavered. He remained confident in His compassion for the kingdom of God.

We need to model this same spirit. How well do you show compassion and kindness to everyone, even your enemies (Luke 6:27-28)? Just as God's kindness leads us to repentance, your kindness, patience, and love (instead of anger and judgment) toward people can powerfully change them.

*Jesus, help me live with the same confidence in
compassion that You showed to everyone
who was needy and hurting.*

Confidence in Victory

*We have troubles all around us, but we are not defeated.
We do not know what to do, but we do not give up the
hope of living. We are persecuted, but God does not leave
us. We are hurt sometimes, but we are not destroyed.*

2 CORINTHIANS 4:8–9 NCV

Christians worldwide are bullied and murdered because of their faith. Even so, we are never without hope in Jesus. Our lives could be taken from us, but we should not fear those who can kill the body but cannot kill the soul (Matthew 10:28). Even in death, there is victory over sin and Satan because we go to be with Jesus (2 Corinthians 5:8).

Heaven is just the beginning. Jesus is coming back for His followers and will defeat Satan, Satan's followers, and death itself. God will create a new heaven and earth where He will live with His people and wipe away every tear. There will be no more death, sadness, crying, or pain. This is the "happily ever after" we eagerly await!

*Lord, help me hold confidently to the hope of
eternal life and Your victory over sin and death.*

Confidence in Christ

I was put to death on the cross with Christ, and I do not live anymore—it is Christ who lives in me. I still live in my body, but I live by faith in the Son of God who loved me and gave himself to save me.

GALATIANS 2:20 NCV

When you live for God, you actually die to yourself. You give up your rights. You understand that your desires don't get to control you, the world doesn't get to tell you what is right or wrong, and others don't get to tell you how you should live. When you belong to Jesus, you lay down your life so Jesus can live through you.

What rights do you cling to? What desires pull you to go your own way? How do you still conform to cultural influences that aren't pleasing to God? You can be confident Christ is living through you when you are growing in love, joy, peace, patience, kindness, goodness, faithfulness, gentleness, and self-control (Galatians 5:22-23). How do you need to die more to yourself today?

Lord, work in my heart so the world can see You clearly through me.

Confidence in the Bible

Because of that experience, we have even greater
confidence in the message proclaimed by the prophets.
You must pay close attention to what they wrote, for their
words are like a lamp shining in a dark place—until the
Day dawns, and Christ the Morning Star shines in your
hearts. Above all, you must realize that no prophecy in
Scripture ever came from the prophet's own understanding,
or from human initiative. No, those prophets were
moved by the Holy Spirit, and they spoke from God.

2 PETER 1:19–21 NLT

Peter's personal experience with Jesus gave him greater confidence in the validity of scripture (2 Peter 1:16–18). You can be confident the message shared in both the Old and New Testaments is from God, not a made-up story from men. Peter witnessed Old Testament prophecy be fulfilled in Jesus, and there are more prophecies yet to be fulfilled. Do you know them? Pay close attention to what the prophets wrote! You can be confident that all of God's prophecies will be fulfilled.

Lord, thank You for Your Word and the road map
it provides. Help me learn and study so I can
be confident as Your return approaches.

Nation Reborn

*"Then you, my people, will know that I am the LORD,
when I open your graves and bring you up from them. I
will put my Spirit in you and you will live, and I will settle
you in your own land. Then you will know that I the LORD
have spoken, and I have done it, declares the LORD."*

EZEKIEL 37:13–14 NIV

In AD 70 the nation of Israel collapsed. Jews despaired of
ever living in the Promised Land again (Ezekiel 37:11). But
more than six hundred years *before* the fall of Jerusalem,
God promised He'd bring their dead nation back to life. The
Balfour Declaration in 1917 allowed Jews to return to their land
(Ezekiel 37:7–8). On May 14, 1948, Israel was officially reborn
as a nation (Ezekiel 37:9–10). No other nation in the history
of the world has disappeared for almost two thousand years
and been reborn. That's the power of God!

God always keeps His promises. If you have any doubts,
you can look at the miracle of Israel.

*Wow, God! If You keep Your word to Israel, I can be
confident You'll keep Your word about everything.*

Now or Later

Yet what we suffer now is nothing compared to the glory he will reveal to us later. For all creation is waiting eagerly for that future day when God will reveal who his children really are. Against its will, all creation was subjected to God's curse. But with eager hope, the creation looks forward to the day when it will join God's children in glorious freedom from death and decay.

ROMANS 8:18-21 NLT

Are you playing a long game or a short game? The short game says, "I don't want to suffer! I'm not going to follow God completely because suffering is overrated. I'll take my paradise now, thanks." The long game says, "It doesn't matter what it costs to follow God. Nothing I suffer now can compare to the future glory I'll receive for my faithfulness and obedience."

Do you have eager hope for the day when we'll be set free from death and decay? Is your confidence in our future reward strong enough to make the present pain worth it?

Lord, help me keep my eyes on the prize and not take the easy way out. If I suffer now, it's worth the reward later.

Stand for Truth

*Looking for a reason to bring charges against Jesus,
they asked him, "Is it lawful to heal on the Sabbath?"
. . . Then he said to the man, "Stretch out your hand."
So he stretched it out and it was completely restored,
just as sound as the other. But the Pharisees went
out and plotted how they might kill Jesus.*

MATTHEW 12:10, 13-14 NIV

The Pharisees' regulations said healing on the Sabbath was
"work," and doing any kind of work on the Sabbath broke the
Law. But Jesus said if a sheep falls into a pit on the Sabbath,
wouldn't even the Pharisees lift it out to rescue it? How much
more valuable is a person than a sheep! It *is* lawful to always
do the right thing, even on the Sabbath (Matthew 12:11–12).

Jesus challenged the religious authorities and the current
status quo. He stood for truth and what was *right*. But standing for truth creates enemies. It did for Jesus, and it will for
you. The truth is not popular. But Jesus didn't back down,
and neither should we.

*Lord, help me confidently share
the truth and do what's right.*

Interrupted

*When Jesus heard what had happened, he withdrew
by boat privately to a solitary place. Hearing of this,
the crowds followed him on foot from the towns.
When Jesus landed and saw a large crowd, he had
compassion on them and healed their sick.*

MATTHEW 14:13–14 NIV

John the Baptist, Jesus' cousin, had been murdered in a brutal
way, and John's disciples had just arrived and informed Jesus
of John's death (Matthew 14:3–12). After hearing the news,
Jesus withdrew to have some private time with His Father.
No doubt Jesus needed a minute to mourn, not to mention
a chance to rest from the physical and emotional exhaustion
of constantly teaching and healing. But the neediness of the
crowd interrupted Jesus' solitude. Instead of ignoring them
or getting angry, He let His compassion for them overrule His
own personal weariness.

Time for personal refreshment is necessary and important,
but when the neediness of others interrupts your solitude,
how do you respond?

*Jesus, I trust You to provide moments of refreshment
when I need it. And when it doesn't seem long enough
or gets interrupted, help me put others' needs above
my own and respond with love and compassion.*

Don't Give Up!

Let us not become weary in doing good,
for at the proper time we will reap a
harvest if we do not give up.
GALATIANS 6:9 NIV

We live in an "instant" culture. Wanna purchase something? Grab your phone and hit "Buy Now" on Amazon! Want some new music? Download it. Food? Pop your instant mac and cheese into the microwave. We're so used to "instant" that when results don't come quickly, we quit. "This isn't going well for me, soooo. . .I'm moving on to something else."

But that's not the attitude Jesus wants us to have. He wants us to develop perseverance. . .to keep praying, keep asking, keep loving. Scripture promises we will reap a harvest if we don't give up. What feels hopeless to you right now? Who are you tempted to give up on? Keep praying and being a light!

Lord, I'm so discouraged. But I'm not quitting. I'm putting
my confidence in Your promise that I'll reap a harvest if I
don't give up. I may not see much fruit now, but that doesn't
mean You're not working and it's not coming. I trust You.

Unstoppable!

"Now I say to you that you are Peter (which means 'rock'), and upon this rock I will build my church, and all the powers of hell will not conquer it."

MATTHEW 16:18 NLT

Who builds the worldwide church and makes it grow? Jesus! Not your church and all its programs. Not you. Jesus declared He's in charge of making sure the church flourishes. He also declared the church is invincible. No amount of evil can ever snuff out or destroy God's people. Persecution of Christians is extremely intense in some countries. But places where governments are killing Christians are also places where the church is growing like wildfire. You can't stop God. And we can live with confidence that God's people will ultimately prevail.

What opposition from the world do you face because of your Christian beliefs? Does it make you feel defeated and hopeless? Or do you find strength from God's unstoppable plan for His church?

Jesus, I pray for Christians worldwide who face horrible persecution. Give them boldness and courage as they stand for truth. Help me also find strength and courage in Your plan for Your people when I face opposition for what I believe.

Reverence and Respect

Fear the LORD your God and serve him.
DEUTERONOMY 10:20 NIV

Have you ever felt that drop in your stomach when you're speeding down the road and spot a hidden police officer? When your principal enters the lunchroom, do students suddenly become less rowdy? How often do you hide something from your parents because you know they'll disapprove? Why do we have these reactions to police officers, principals, and parents? Because we *fear* them. We recognize their authority, and we recognize there is an expected standard of behavior and consequences if the rules are broken.

The Bible commands us many times to fear God (Deuteronomy 6:13, 24; 10:12; 31:12, 13). The fear of God is meant to keep us from sinning (Exodus 1:17; 20:20; Leviticus 19:14; 25:17, 43). It provides a healthy dose of respect so we give God the honor and reverence He deserves. God is loving, yes! His grace is plentiful, yes! But we must also respect His authority. How do you fear God? How do you need to show Him more reverence?

Lord, help me have a healthy respect for Your authority.
Help my reverence for You guide my behavior.

All-Sufficient God

That evening the disciples came to him and said, "This is a remote place, and it's already getting late. Send the crowds away so they can go to the villages and buy food for themselves." But Jesus said, "That isn't necessary—you feed them." "But we have only five loaves of bread and two fish!" they answered. "Bring them here," he said.

MATTHEW 14:15-18 NLT

The disciples recognized the urgent need of the crowd to eat—perhaps the disciples' own stomachs were rumbling!—and had compassion on them. But Jesus commanded His disciples to feed the crowd. The disciples swiftly understood they did not have the resources to complete such a task. Jesus simply asked them to give what they had. Jesus took their meager offering, blessed it, and fed more than five thousand people with it (Matthew 14:19-21)!

When Jesus commands us to do something, we often feel insufficient—because we are! Just offer what you have, and let our all-sufficient God bless it and multiply it.

God, I often lack confidence about my ability. But it's not about what I bring. It's about trusting how big and capable You are!

Trust Training

Immediately after this, Jesus insisted that his disciples get back into the boat and cross to the other side of the lake, while he sent the people home. After sending them home, he went up into the hills by himself to pray. Night fell while he was there alone. Meanwhile, the disciples were in trouble far away from land, for a strong wind had risen, and they were fighting heavy waves.

MATTHEW 14:22–24 NLT

Immediately after the disciples finished feeding the crowd, Jesus put them on a boat. "If Jesus is all-knowing, didn't He know He was sending them into a dangerous storm?" you ask. Yep! "Wait, wait, wait. . .so Jesus *knowingly* and *purposefully* sent His disciples into a terrifying storm while He stayed behind?" Yes.

God allows us to struggle with circumstances too big for us to handle in order to teach us to trust Him. Jesus came to His disciples during the storm, offering His peace and His presence (Matthew 14:25–27). He never abandons us, but He will train us to trust Him.

Jesus, when I feel abandoned, help me recognize that You aren't forsaking me; You're training me. Help me trust You.

Weakness Is Power

Each time he said, "My grace is all you need. My power works best in weakness." So now I am glad to boast about my weaknesses, so that the power of Christ can work through me. That's why I take pleasure in my weaknesses, and in the insults, hardships, persecutions, and troubles that I suffer for Christ. For when I am weak, then I am strong.

2 CORINTHIANS 12:9–10 NLT

Look back through the last couple of devotions. How did the disciples' weakness magnify Jesus' power? We often feel like we need to be Super Christians—bold and confident and have all the answers. But when we're operating in our own strength, we get in the way of God's glory. God shines best when we're at our worst.

How easy is it for you to admit your weaknesses? How is God asking you to surrender and to trust His power and strength today?

Lord, I must become less so You can show Yourself greater. Help me be confident in my weakness because, really, that's when You show Your strength.

Blessed Suffering

And since we are his children, we are his heirs. In fact,
together with Christ we are heirs of God's glory. But if we
are to share his glory, we must also share his suffering.

ROMANS 8:17 NLT

Jesus said, "The thief's purpose is to steal and kill and destroy.
My purpose is to give them a rich and satisfying life" (John 10:10
NLT). We often read this verse and interpret it to mean that
God's plan is to bless us with health, wealth, and prosperity;
we are meant to experience an easy life filled with God's
abundant blessings!

But God's Word promises we'll experience blessing *and*
suffering. Both. Did Jesus lead a rich and satisfying life? Yes,
He did. Did He also suffer? Yes, terribly. What if your suffering
is the blessing? What if the richness God desires to give you
must be obtained through tough circumstances? A blessed
life does not mean an easy life. How does your perspective
need to change?

Lord, forgive me for believing life should be easy
and for getting angry with You when it's not.

Spiritual Exercise

The Lord will make you go through hard times, but he himself will be there to teach you, and you will not have to search for him any more. If you wander off the road to the right or the left, you will hear his voice behind you saying, "Here is the road. Follow it."

ISAIAH 30:20-21 GNT

Your trust in God will not strengthen until you're in situations where you *have* to trust Him—and He proves Himself to you. The Lord *wants* you to have strong faith. So He will allow you to go through hard things. Just like exercise builds strong muscles, life's difficulties build a strong faith. Exercise makes you sore, and hard times hurt. But how you respond to the pain matters. Do you get angry, pushing God away? Or are you teachable, seeking His purpose in the pain and depending on Him? You can be confident that every tough situation in your life is meant to strengthen you—and that Jesus is there guiding you through it.

Lord, thank You for loving me enough to push me and grow my faith and for staying by my side to lead me through it.

Perfecting Faith

*Let us look only to Jesus, the One who began
our faith and who makes it perfect.*

HEBREWS 12:2 NCV

The Bible clearly states God chose us before we could choose
Him (John 6:44; Ephesians 1:4). His gentle leading guided
us to salvation and the beginning of our faith. Now that you
are rooted in Him, He will perfect your faith. He knows your
weaknesses. He also knows His plans for you—and the level
of faith required to accomplish those plans. God will continue
to nurture your faith in a way that's specific to you. That
means He'll test you in ways He might not test others. He'll
put you through trials others may not have to endure. He'll
shape and build your faith perfectly for the journey He has
planned for you.

Keep your eyes fixed firmly on Jesus—not someone else
and how great or easy she has it. How are you tempted to
compare your faith journey with someone else's?

*Lord, thank You for the trials and temptations
that are perfecting my faith. Help me stay
focused on You and not be distracted with
someone else's journey compared to mine.*

Pride Check

*This is the confidence that we have through Christ
in the presence of God. It isn't that we ourselves
are qualified to claim that anything came from
us. No, our qualification is from God.*

2 CORINTHIANS 3:4–5 CEB

Are you really smart? Super athletic? An amazing artist? It's easy to take pride in our natural abilities. "I'm really good at that. [Blows on nails and buffs them on shirt.] Yeah, I know. Keep the praise coming!" It's super tempting to be confident in ourselves because of our abilities. But who gave you those abilities? God! He's the source of all your talents—and He deserves all the praise for your talents.

When God calls you to do something that's beyond your natural talents, you can put your confidence in Him. If He's asked you to do it, He'll equip you and qualify you to get it done. So whether you're operating from gifts that come naturally to you or you've stepped outside your comfort zone and are fully depending on God—it's God who deserves the honor and praise!

*Lord, help me use the talents You've given
me to give You glory and not seek my own.*

On Again, Off Again

"But the people soon forgot about the LORD their God, so he handed them over to. . .the king of Moab, who fought against them. Then they cried to the LORD again and confessed, 'We have sinned by turning away from the LORD and worshiping the images of Baal and Ashtoreth. But we will worship you and you alone if you will rescue us from our enemies.'"

1 SAMUEL 12:9–10 NLT

How many times do you desperately run to God for help, then after He provides, you go right back to ignoring Him? Truly following God means complete dedication. He is not pleased when we run to Him with empty plea bargains so we can escape the consequences of our actions: "God, if You save me, I promise I'll start reading my Bible every day and going to church every week." He desires a genuinely repentant heart that turns away from sin.

What habits, people, apps, or situations tempt you to turn away from the Lord? What needs to be sacrificed so you can follow God with your whole heart?

God, I'm sorry for ignoring You.
Help me follow You with my whole heart.

Truth Redefined

But God shows his anger from heaven against all
sinful, wicked people who suppress the truth by their
wickedness. . . . Yes, they knew God, but they wouldn't
worship him as God or even give him thanks. And they
began to think up foolish ideas of what God was like.
As a result, their minds became dark and confused.
. . . They traded the truth about God for a lie.
ROMANS 1:18, 21, 25 NLT

How does rebellion against God begin? By suppressing the truth. If truth can be changed, redefined, or made relative, then sinful desires can be justified and made acceptable. Next, rebellion progresses to outright rejection of God—dishonoring Him and refusing to thank Him for anything. How do you see the evidence of rebellion in our culture today? How have people exchanged the truth about God for a lie?

How are you tempted to suppress the truth? The Bible clearly defines who God is and what He commands. What's hard for you to accept? How do you attempt to redefine God and His standards?

Lord, rebellion surrounds me. Help me recognize the
lies our culture peddles and stand firm in Your truth.

Extreme Measures

"So if your hand or foot causes you to sin, cut it off and throw it away. It's better to enter eternal life with only one hand or one foot than to be thrown into eternal fire with both of your hands and feet. And if your eye causes you to sin, gouge it out and throw it away. It's better to enter eternal life with only one eye than to have two eyes and be thrown into the fire of hell."

MATTHEW 18:8-9 NLT

Jesus used strong figurative language to make a point: extreme measures should be taken to cut sin out of our lives. Sin is serious. But we grow comfortable with it. We ignore it and justify it. Maintaining the status quo is never more important than following God.

What personal sin do you let slide? Do you easily fall into gossip with certain friends? Do you lie to protect yourself from getting in trouble? What extreme measures do you need to take? Stop associating with certain friends? Close your social media accounts? Remove apps from your devices?

Lord, help me take sin seriously.
What changes do I need to make?

Habit of Forgiveness

Peter came up to the Lord and asked, "How many times should I forgive someone who does something wrong to me? Is seven times enough?" Jesus answered: "Not just 7 times, but 77 times!"

MATTHEW 18:21-22 CEV

Jewish teachers during Jesus' time said you were required to extend forgiveness only three times. Peter thought he was being more than generous forgiving someone *seven* times. But Jesus extended the threshold even further. Jesus didn't literally mean seventy-seven times, like we're supposed to tally each time we forgive. After all, love keeps no record of wrongs (1 Corinthians 13:5). We need to forgive someone an infinite number of times.

Jesus told a story to illustrate His point in Matthew 18:23-34. No offense against us outweighs the immensity of our personal sin against God. He has forgiven us, so we need to forgive others. Who do you struggle to forgive? What offenses still bother you? What steps toward forgiveness and reconciliation does God want you to take?

Jesus, help me love and forgive like You. Change my perspective so I can have a forgiving heart toward others, knowing how much I have been forgiven by You.

Keep Choosing Confidence

So do not throw away this confident trust in the Lord. Remember the great reward it brings you!

HEBREWS 10:35 NLT

It's been a journey! You've taken a closer look at who God is and His worthiness of our confidence. You explored who you are in Christ and the confidence that gives you. You've reflected on numerous things the Bible has to say about confidence. How has your confidence grown since the beginning of this devotional?

Take some time to reflect on all that you've learned, how much you've grown, and how much more confident you are. Hold the lessons you've learned close. They're treasures of great value! When you're tempted to doubt and waver in your trust, remember the great reward your confidence has brought you. Let it bolster your faith and encourage your heart. Continue to be a girl of faith and choose confidence!

Lord, thank You for all You've taught me through this devotional. When I face tough moments in the future, help me not to throw away my confident trust in You—but to remember the truths and lessons You've taught me and the great reward I've experienced by trusting You.

About the Author

April Frazier has published more than fifty articles in national magazines and book anthologies such as *Guideposts for Teens*, *Brio & Beyond*, and *God's Way for Teens*. She coauthored *3-Minute Devotions for Teen Girls* and *3-Minute Devotions for Teen Guys*. She graduated from Bethel University in Mishawaka, Indiana, with degrees in English and Biblical Literature. She went on to earn a Master of Theology in Christian Education and Bible Exposition at Dallas Theological Seminary. You can find her doing crazy things like sugaring (tapping maple trees and making homemade maple syrup), homeschooling her three children, and fermenting kimchi. Her favorite activities are exploring antique stores with her husband, reading, hiking, and horseback riding in the woods. Find her on Facebook at www.facebook.com/AprilFrazierAuthor.